MW00633954

CAREER RECOVERY

CAREER RECOVERY

Creating Hopeful Careers in Difficult Times

Spencer Niles, Norman Amundson,
Roberta Neault, & Hyung Joon Yoon

cognella®

SAN DIEGO

Bassim Hamadeh, CEO and Publisher
Amy Smith, Senior Project Editor
Alia Bales, Production Editor
Emely Villavicencio, Senior Graphic Designer
Alexa Lucido, Licensing Manager
Natalie Piccotti, Director of Marketing
Kassie Graves, Vice President of Editorial
Jamie Giganti, Director of Academic Publishing

Copyright © 2021 by Spencer Niles, Norman Amundson, Roberta Neault, and Hyung Joon Yoon.
All rights reserved. No part of this publication may be reprinted, reproduced, transmitted, or
utilized in any form or by any electronic, mechanical, or other means, now known or hereafter
invented, including photocopying, microfilming, and recording, or in any information retrieval
system without the written permission of Cognella, Inc. For inquiries regarding permissions,
translations, foreign rights, audio rights, and any other forms of reproduction, please contact
the Cognella Licensing Department at rights@cognella.com.

Trademark Notice: Product or corporate names may be trademarks or registered trademarks
and are used only for identification and explanation without intent to infringe.

This book was previously published by Pearson Education, Inc.

Cover image copyright © 2019 iStockphoto LP/Oleksandr Pupko.

Printed in the United States of America.

cognella ACADEMIC PUBLISHING
3970 Sorrento Valley Blvd., Ste. 500, San Diego, CA 92121

BRIEF CONTENTS

DETAILED CONTENTS

PREFACE

his book provides a model that you can use throughout you lifetime to guide you in career planning. The model we introduce is one that has been tested and used with a variety of populations as diverse as university students, Syrian refugees, unemployed workers, and many others throughout the world.

Career Recovery emphasizes the Hope-Action Theory. Hope-Action Theory offers strategies that can guide your career- even in these difficult times. Having a strategy that is proven and tested in some of the most challenging situations, such as Hope-Action Theory, provides confidence that, by using the steps we discuss in this book, (steps you can use throughout your life) you can take ownership of your career development.

Also in Section I by addressing the challenges workers experience today. As you know very well, they are substantial. Yet, even in these difficult times, there are strategies you can use to both take care of yourself and to construct a career that you find meaningful. To move forward in this way, we all need to have a sense of hope. Hope is crucial to gaining momentum in your career planning. We explain how you can generate and sustain a sense of hope in your life and work

In Section I, we introduce the essential aspects of Hope-Action Theory. In Chapter 1, we discuss the challenges of effective career self-management in the post-pandemic period. We also discuss strategies for creating a sense of hope even in the most challenging times. More specifically, in Chapter 2, we introduce the importance of hope in the career planning process. This content provides the foundation for Section II, which opens with Chapter 3 in which we provide an introductory overview to the key competencies comprising the Hope-Action Theory.

Section II also provides a more in-depth look into the crucial process of engaging in self-reflection to develop self-clarity. This process provides a solid foundation for all effective career self-management. The chapters of Section II guide readers through deeper self-exploration and address the topics of passions, skills, personal style, and values (Chapters 4–7).

Section III represents a turning point in the book. It begins with Chapter 8 highlighting the need for support (e.g., emotional, informational, and financial) in career and educational planning. Support, the common factor emerging in almost all research related to resilience, gets people through challenging times and helps them maintain their engagement in the challenging processes of the post-pandemic period. The steps discussed (vision, goal setting, and planning) in Chapters 9 and 10 are the points in the Hope-Action Theory when the primarily inward process of self-exploration turns outward as you learn how to connect self-information to future possibilities.

Section IV moves even more deeply into outward action via the process of connecting to the world-of-work, implementing decisions and turning possibilities into realities (Chapters 12 and 13, respectively). More specifically, this section begins with a focus in Chapter 11 on connecting to possibilities through occupational research, integrating self-assessment data, learning how to communicate career goals to others, and making use of trend spotting in career self-management. Chapter 12 highlights how to intentionally make the most of the opportunities connected to career and educational goals. Chapter 13 guides you as you turn possibilities into realities through effective job searching. Chapter 14 addresses how to generate job leads and work opportunities. We also describe how you can refine job interview skills and develop social support in the job search process. Finally, Section IV concludes (Chapter 15) by teaching you how to use the new information you learned about yourself and occupations as they engage in the ongoing process to manage you careers effectively—even in difficult times.

In essence, the book ends by returning to the beginning (self-reflection to develop self-clarity). This cyclical process highlights two essential facts: (a) The self evolves, thus, we are continually making choices and adjusting to the choices we make, and (b) the world of work also evolves over time, making choosing and adjusting to one's choices continuous requirements. Toward those realities, the Hope-Action Theory is a model that you can use throughout your lifetime to engage in productive career self-management.

INTRODUCTION TO HOPE-ACTION THEORY

1 | CAREER RECOVERY DURING THE PANDEMIC

OBJECTIVES

This chapter focuses on the importance of recovering from the trauma occurring during the COVID-19 pandemic. We introduce the concepts of "positive uncertainty," the experience of trauma, and the Hope-Action Theory as starting places for career recovery. After reading and completing activities in this chapter, you will be able to do the following:

- Understand how the pandemic experience created career trauma

- Understand the importance of positive uncertainty and hope in career recovery

CASE EXAMPLE

Ruth, age 52, was doing well. She would say that she had finally hit her stride and was feeling as though she were in her prime. She was working in her dream job and helping to provide a good income for her family. Ruth worked as a pilot for one of the largest airlines in the world. In every way, Ruth was the consummate professional. Highly respected for both her skill as a pilot and her care for her coworkers, this mother of two felt truly blessed. Ruth and her husband, Alex, owned a lovely home in an Atlanta suburb. Alex worked as a manager for a very well-known hotel chain. Their jobs provided a substantial income with great benefits, including the chance for the family to take marvelous vacations throughout the world.

Most would say that Ruth and Alex had it all. Then, people started falling ill. At first, it seemed like the typical flu, but later it became clear that it was much worse. The mother of a flight attendant whom Ruth worked with suddenly passed away after being ill for a week. Another colleague's brother went into intensive care and was placed on a ventilator. Similar stories emerged of people falling ill, some missing work for a week or so, others faring much worse. Then reality hit. This was no ordinary flu. This was much, much worse. An apparent deadly illness for which there was no cure. Within days, news reports included terms like "pandemic," "coronavirus," and "COVID-19." Workers were sent home, not knowing if they would have a job to return to once the pandemic was under control. While worked stopped, bills continued, and many experienced substantial financial challenges.

Overriding all of this was the abiding fear of contracting the virus. Devastating stories of people who were healthy one day and placed in intensive care the next day commonly appeared in the news. The most tragic outcomes were those who not only died but died alone as their family members were barred from being with their loved ones due to the need to contain the virus's spread. Despite how well things had been going for Ruth and Alex, they were not immune to the pandemic's fallout. People stopped flying, and hotel occupancies came to a screeching halt. Not only were Ruth and Alex worried about staying healthy, but they were also worried about paying their bills. Alex was laid off first. Then, Ruth's work schedule was substantially reduced. Although they had some savings, they worried how long those would last. Things felt like they were crumbling in a hurry. As part of his benefits package, Alex was invited to meet with a career coach. He wasn't sure what help the coach could be, but he was worried and not sure how to move forward. He felt numb, stuck, and hopeless.

Although the details may vary, the themes are the same—millions of workers worried about staying healthy, paying bills, and whether they would be able to survive the storm known as the COVID-19 pandemic. Everything changed in a few short weeks. Unemployment numbers exploded, and although the government worked to find ways to help, for many, the help was either too slow in arriving or too little to make a difference. Against this backdrop, having a sense of hope for the future seemed impossible. Yet giving up, whether or not you had the virus or lost a job, meant the pandemic won. What Alex needed was a way to navigate the storm. Some strategies for identifying and considering his options. And the chance to connect with others dealing with the same challenges. With this book, we offer strategies that you can use to navigate any career challenge you confront. Given all that is going on today, that is a bold statement. Yet, it is true. With a strategy, you can create a plan that makes sense. Without a strategy, you could feel like a small boat lost in a raging sea.

During the pandemic, most people found themselves lamenting about the economy. *What about the job crisis?* many would wonder. It was a common phrase uttered by many who saw it just too overwhelming to comprehend how our society had been shaken by the current health and economic crisis. A huge and tragic double whammy. The global spread of the COVID-19 virus was unexpected and devastating in every possible way. It would be great to think that we could just go back to the way things were, but that seemed hard to imagine. The pandemic brought a new reality and a new "normal." There was no denying or avoiding that fact. Many were struggling to deal with what had happened, cope with the shock, figure out a way to rebalance, and figure out a way to keep moving. The trauma was real, and getting through it would take some time and support. That is exactly what Ruth and Alex were struggling with when Alex went to meet his career coach for the first time.

For this kind of career recovery to occur, we need to start with mustering a sense of hope and determination, a resolve to get through the crisis and emerge with a new sense of direction and purpose. Most of us have encountered significant challenges in our lives before the pandemic. We've been through tough times before, and what we learned from those experiences will serve us well in the current crisis. One of the first challenges to address is the fact that, like all crises, many things are uncertain. Ambiguity is one of the most challenging things for people to cope with, but uncertainty does not have to lead to ambivalence. We need to remind ourselves of the coping strategies we used in the past, draw on our resources, learn new resources, and keep moving forward.

The decision-making expert H. B. Gelatt talked about the need to develop a stance of "positive uncertainty" toward our decisions. Certainty is what makes you comfortable; uncertainty is what makes you creative. Both are useful. Ruth and Alex experienced a substantial and unexpected upheaval in their lives. Seeking some degree of certainty and stability in the form of definitive answers to the questions they were asking (e.g., "Will we survive?" "What job will I do if I can't do this one?" "How will we pay our bills?") is important and makes perfect sense. They need to develop solutions to these essential questions. In looking at their futures and considering new possibilities, however, positive uncertainty can open the door to creative and new solutions to next steps taken in the current context. Their creativity can lead them to identifying the next opportunity.

Positive uncertainty also involves responding to situations with a sense of excitement rather than fear. In this book, we provide resources you can use to generate more excitement than worry about your current and future situation. We offer a structure that you can quickly learn and readily apply in navigating any career challenge you encounter. The concepts we teach in this book are grounded in years of research and our work with thousands of people in similar situations as you. We are eager to help and honored to join you on this journey.

Let's start by saying a little about hope (more in the next chapter). Hope represents the core of what we will discuss throughout the book. The type of hope that we focus on, however, is not hope in the sense of wishful thinking. Wishful thinking is helpful but not long-lasting and not likely to help too much when you encounter challenges in your career. Wishful thinking fades away amid those challenges. Instead, we focus on hope that is grounded in action. When you take steps that are intentional and goal-directed, then you begin to experience something very different. You start to believe that there are actually things you can do to improve your situation. You begin to generate a sense of hope. This type of action-oriented hope drives the model we will teach you, which is called Hope-Action Theory. This model is grounded in hope and contains a set of competencies that, collectively, provide you with the structure you can rely on to manage your career effectively throughout your lifetime—no matter what challenges you encounter.

Weathering the Storm

The first step of the journey is to acknowledge and recognize what you have just gone through and what you are continuing to go through. If you have lost your job, you are no doubt in a swirl. In talking with people about their experience of being unemployed, they often speak about "being in the storm," "being blindsided," finding themselves "up in the air," "falling off a cliff," being "lost in a fog," or having their "legs kicked out from under them." Using metaphors to describe your experience is often an excellent way to provide a new perspective on your experience. Naming what you are experiencing is an excellent first step in beginning to deal with it constructively.

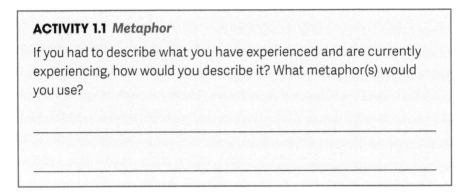

ACTIVITY 1.1 *Metaphor*

If you had to describe what you have experienced and are currently experiencing, how would you describe it? What metaphor(s) would you use?

_____

_____

While these images are all somewhat different, they do have something in common. They suggest that we have gone through some form of **trauma**. Trauma is a deeply distressing or disturbing experience, and it is associated with a variety of emotional responses, some of which include:

> shock, denial, disbelief, confusion, distraction, anger, irritability, anxiety, fear, self-blame, withdrawal, hopelessness, despair, numbness, grief, disorientation

Because the pandemic was unforeseen by most of us, feeling any of these emotions (or all of them) is normal. The pandemic was unexpected and gave people little opportunity for any type of preparation. It also was quite unlike anything that we have experienced during the globalized age (Philp, 2020).

When considering this extensive range of reactions, it is essential to recognize that there is a great deal of variability in how people perceive their situation, how they react to it, and how they cope with the experience. We all respond differently depending on our circumstances, our disposition, and our past experiences. What is common is that both our thoughts and our feelings are involved as we attempt to come to terms with what has happened. Our reactions are normal and to be expected under the circumstances.

It is one thing to have a traumatic experience and then to get back to our regular life patterns, but this event has changed our lives in so many ways. In many respects, we will continue to carry this with us for years to come. What makes this situation unique is the fact that coupled with the trauma-related physical threat of the virus, there is also the actual experience of being unemployed or underemployed experienced by millions of people.

There has been considerable research exploring the impact of unemployment and underemployment on mental and physical well-being (Moser, 2009). The research findings are consistent in showing the potential for a decline in physical and psychological health. Unemployment offers a set of unique challenges (loss reactions), and underemployment can negatively impact one's self-confidence and readiness for change. Unemployment can also lead to an emotional roller-coaster–type of experience (Borgen & Amundson, 1987). Something positive can occur that brightens your spirits and pulls you up. If that experience is not what you were hoping for, however, it can lead to a rapid downward emotional swing and further discouragement can set in. This emotional roller-coaster experience incorporates aspects of both loss and burnout reactions.

It is essential when viewing these reactions to fully understand that they are a normal response to a challenging situation. They will occur, and they can present a barrier, but they can also be overcome, and they won't last forever. It is understandable when our basic human needs are being undermined that we will have some type of reaction. Basic human needs include the need for financial security, the need for relationships and community, the need for a structure to our life, and the need for meaning and purpose in what we are doing. The storm or turbulence in our lives can be disorienting and disruptive. Still, it is possible to recover our sense of balance and hope, to fashion a new perspective on what is happening around us, to apply our creative and intellectual capacity to generate new possibilities, and to reset our resolve to move forward. We are eager to guide you through these experiences toward a better, more positive, and more hopeful place. We are confident you can achieve all these things and more.

Our Hope-Action Theory approach is laid out in the next chapter and this is what most of the rest of the book is all about. We place **HOPE** at the center point of career development and use a pinwheel diagram to describe the various competencies that help power our sense of hopefulness. Please read on! The journey is just beginning.

Questions for Reflection and Discussion

1. Take a close look at the metaphor image you put down at the beginning of this chapter. How could you change the image so that it is more positive and hopeful? You can stick with the image you put down or create something different.

2. If you take a "positive uncertainty" stance in going forward, how might that influence your actions and your general well-being?

References

Borgen, W. A., & Amundson, N. E. (1987). The dynamics of unemployment. *Journal of Counseling and Development, 66,* 180–184. https://doi.org/10.1002/j.1556-6676.1987.tb00841.x

Moser, P. K. (2009). Unemployment impairs mental health: Meta-analyses. *Journal of Vocational Behavior, 74,* 264–282. https://doi.org/10.1016/j.jvb.2009.01.001

Philp, C. (2020, April 9). How coronavirus will change the world forever. *The Times of London.* https://www.thetimes.co.uk/article/how-coronavirus-will-change-the-world-for-ever-2fj5h5f8p

CREATING HOPE

2

OBJECTIVES

This chapter focuses on the importance of hope in career planning. We introduce the Hope-Action Theory as a strategy for creating and sustaining hope in your career development. After reading and completing activities in this chapter, you will be able to do the following:

- Understand the importance of hope

- Understand how to generate and sustain hope in your career

CASE EXAMPLE

Alice met with her career coach to discuss her job loss. She had worked with an accounting firm since her senior year of college. Despite feeling sad and angry about losing her job due to the COVID-19 pandemic, deep down she was also scared. Alice knew that she often found her workdays boring and not challenging. She originally expected to find each day to be enjoyable and meaningful. She had landed a job that connected directly to her college major. Things were looking good! Although she experienced many positive moments at work, there were also moments that were anything but positive. She often wondered: Is this how it was supposed to be? Did her negative experiences mean that she had chosen the wrong career? She felt panic as she considered these questions while walking to meet with her career coach for the first time since losing her job. Although she had entered her job full of hope, she exited it with more questions than answers, with her hope in doubt, and with a myriad of feelings she was having trouble sorting through.

lice's first work experience was a bit of a "shocker" from start to finish. She was particularly rattled by the finish. Several months before, she was making plans for vacation and she and her fiancé were considering buying a home together. COVID-19 changed everything, however. As she attempted to adjust to her new reality, she had a host of questions. Although there were positive aspects to her job, there were a good many less-than-positive experiences. And the unexpected ending shook her confidence and her hope.

At the start of her work, she was excited and looked forward to the work she would do. She had hoped that her experience would reinforce her choice of career. What she had not planned for were the challenges that she encountered long before the virus changed things. Alice was having trouble integrating these experiences into her overall understanding of what a work experience should be like. In essence, she had expected things to flow much more smoothly. She was shaken by "the rough waters" she encountered and their implications for her future plans. Were they signs of a poor career choice? Were they indications of "issues" that she needed to address to become a better prospective employee? What should she think at this point and what should she do? Especially now. Where she had been hopeful, she now was concerned, skeptical, and questioning her choices. Moreover, she is unclear as to what she should do next and her hopefulness has been replaced by worry. Maybe most importantly, she felt betrayed. She had worked hard, been productive, earned positive reviews, yet here she was. Unemployed.

In her first meeting with her career coach, Alice was invited to share what she was feeling. She was reluctant to discuss her feelings at first. Part of her wasn't sure she could handle all that she was feeling. As she started to share, however, her feelings began flowing out. Underneath all her feelings was a sense of fear and confusion. Although she was grateful for the unemployment money she would receive, that obviously was only a short-term solution. She felt that everything was "up in the air" and she wanted to reconsider everything about her career. She also shared that it felt good to talk about what she was experiencing. Her career coach shared that she had worked with many people in the situation Alice was in and that what she was feeling was very normal and typical.

Alice is in a very challenging situation. She is having doubts about her career choice and at the same time dealing with the current economic trauma and the challenge of unemployment. Her metaphor of being "up in the air" captures some of the ways in which she is experiencing this upheaval. Both trauma and unemployment research point to cognitive and emotional instability. Under these conditions people are often feeling confused, fearful, disoriented, and anxious. They are second guessing themselves and doubting their own abilities. Some of these reactions are reflective of what has been called an "emotional roller coaster" (Borgen & Amundson, 1987). Under these conditions it is not surprising that Alice is having questions about her career choice. These questions need to be taken seriously, but at the same time, it is important to recognize the context in which these concerns have arisen.

Responding to the questions depends, to a great degree, on how you conceptualize career development. Many times people think about work the same way that they think about relationships. Specifically, that difficult times suggest that one has made a poor choice in a partner or, in Alice's instance, a career. Although that can be true, it would be unrealistic to expect one's work (and one's relationships) to always be blissful and positive. In all careers, there are challenges and rewards. There are times when things go smoothly, perhaps even effortlessly. There are other times, however, when it feels like a constant uphill struggle. There are times of excitement and times of boredom. Thus, in managing your career effectively it is important to be able to handle the positive and the challenging aspects of your work. Alice was struggling with determining which challenges she experienced were normal and which were indications that she had made a poor choice. She also was experiencing unemployment for the first time since college. Her career coach shared what she could expect regarding her recovery from losing her job. The coach assured her that she would recover. That through support, and by using a systematic approach to considering her situation, it would be possible for Alice to not only survive but even, eventually, to thrive. Alice felt supported and understood by her coach. Maybe it would be possible for her to recover, she thought tentatively.

Why Is Hope Important?

Most of us have experienced times when we did not feel very hopeful about our lives. See if you can recall a *specific* experience when you lacked hope, perhaps even felt hopeless. Try to imagine, just for a moment, the details of that experience. What happened to shake your hopefulness? Like Alice, you may have tried out something and then learned some things about the choice you made that were not what you expected or that you even liked. These experiences may have led you to become unsure about yourself and your career. Continue focusing on your specific hope-challenged experience. How did you feel about yourself in that moment? How confident were you at that time in your ability to do things successfully? What questions did it lead you to ask about yourself and your situation? What was your energy level? Did you feel stuck? Maybe immobilized? Lacking in motivation? Did you lack a sense of direction and purpose in that moment? When our hope is low, these reactions are all possible experiences. Such experiences can derail our momentum and lead us to ask serious questions about who we are and what we want. In the worst case, we can become depressed and feel unable to move forward. In such instances, we sometimes feel as though these more negative feelings will stay with us forever and that there is nothing we can do to shake them. We want our situation and our feelings to shift toward something more positive, but we might not have a strategy for creating this positive change in our lives.

We want you to know that there are proven steps you can take to make positive changes when you experience moments of hopelessness. You can use these steps to increase your hope, identify a goal, chart a direction, and move forward toward your goal with confidence and purpose. There is no superpower required to make this happen! The steps are easy to learn and practice. And, once learned, they will be helpful to you for the rest of your life.

Our goal in this book is to teach you these steps that will help you address any career challenge you will encounter, now and in the future. These steps, which anyone can learn, will feel like a superpower, but, as we noted, they really are not. Having said that, if by using them you feel more confident, more directed, happier, energized, motivated, and like you have a real sense of purpose in your life, then, well, maybe they are steps to a superpower!

A key to having these positive experiences is to understand the nature of hope and why hope is so important.

Research evidence consistently demonstrates that hope is associated with a number of positive outcomes across cultures. Specifically, high hope has been correlated with high levels of job performance, sports performance, organizational commitment, job satisfaction, clarity in career decision making, overall confidence, and academic achievement, to mention just a few of the ways in which hope is important in our lives. Conversely, lack of hope has been correlated with high levels of absenteeism from school and work, disengagement from academics, and higher levels of dropping out of school. So, having a way to create and sustain a sense of hope in your life is a big deal!

There are, however, many interpretations of the term "hope." Merriam-Webster Dictionary (n.d.) defines hope as "a desire accompanied by expectation of, or belief in, fulfillment." Hope has been conceptualized in a variety of ways in the counseling literature. For example, Diemer and Blustein (2007) defined career-related hope as involving a person's commitment to the notion of career and to working in the future, despite experiencing external barriers. Diemer and Blustein's definition includes having a psychological commitment to working despite the challenges one may encounter in their career development. Others conceptualize hope as a "multidimensional life force characterized by confident yet uncertain expectations of achieving a future good" (Dufault & Martochhio, 1985, p. 380). Averill, Catlin, and Chon (1990) conceptualize hope as primarily an emotion rather than a cognitive construct. Similarly, Bruininks and Malle (2005) conceptualize hope as an emotion that occurs when an individual is focused on an important positive future outcome, over which he or she has little (but still some) personal control.

Our definition of hope is based on the work of the late Rick Snyder (1994, 2002). Snyder, a clinical psychologist, was one of the world's leading hope researchers. In Snyder's approach to hope, he perceived success (both formative and summative success) related to goal pursuit as leading to positive emotions and, conversely, failure leading to negative emotions. High hope people respond differently than low hope people when they encounter impediments to goal achievement. High hope individuals typically respond more positively in such instances (i.e., they are more like to persist toward goal achievement) because they can identify alternative ways to achieve their goals and can adjust their strategies for goal achievement as necessary, while low hope individuals are less successful in this regard (Snyder, 1994). With this in mind, Snyder (2002) defined hope as "the perceived capability to derive pathways to desired goals, and motivate oneself via agency thinking to use those pathways" (p. 249). According to this theory, hopeful individuals are more likely to have practical goals for their lives. Moreover, they are able to find different ways to pursue their goals and, importantly, they take sustained actions toward goal achievement. Thus, in Snyder's model, hope is comprised of three primary components: (a) a goal (or anchor points), (b) thoughts (or pathways) about how to achieve those goals, and (c) the confidence and willingness (agency) to achieve those goals. So, Snyder (2002) conceptualized hope as "primarily a way of thinking, with feelings playing an important, albeit contributory role" (p. 249).

Snyder's definition of hope is very different than the more common belief that hope is simply wishful thinking. Undoubtedly, you have heard someone say something like "I hope things turn out okay." There is nothing wrong with wishing for positive outcomes. Jiminy Cricket told Pinocchio that "when you wish upon a star your dreams come true." Unfortunately, just wishing for an outcome rarely generates the outcome you desire. More usually some action has to happen for the positive outcomes you desire to become a reality. Wishing thinking just by itself is far too passive. It suggests that there is nothing for you to do to increase the probability of a desired outcome occurring. That is not the sort of hope we suggest you rely on. Rather, we recommend a view that aligns with Snyder's, which is much more action oriented. In this approach, you must be motivated to take intentional actions to achieve an important and specific goal.

ACTIVITY 2.1 *Goal Identification*

Rather than continuing to read at this point, we ask that you take time to identify a specific goal that is important to you, one that will require some effort on your part but also one that you have a realistic probability of achieving in the next month.

Goals are important because they provide a purpose and direction for you. It is the difference between getting in your car and driving with no destination in mind and having a clear destination in mind. Once you identify a goal you have a direction to move toward. Goals anchor purposive behavior.

Goals can be short term or long term. They can big (for example, to earn a PhD) or small (to be well prepared for an exam next week). They must, however, be important to you. An important goal should be connected to your values. Try to identify the values that are embedded in the goal you just identified. Values can be things such as making a positive difference in the world; helping others; earning a high income; using abilities; having time for family and friends; living in a healthy way (exercising, eating right, etc.); being in charge of your time; traveling; having a family; being creative; academic achievement; prestige; working hard; doing things that are interesting to you; following rules; and so on. Knowing which values are most important to you is important. Your goals should connect to your important values whenever this is possible; otherwise, it will not be a goal that you care about and you will not be motivated to achieve it. That said, it is true that some goals only connect to your values indirectly. For example, some people struggle with taking general education courses in college because they do not see a direct connection to their interests and goals. In most instances, however, these courses are required for graduation. In these situations, the best some can do is to understand that while a particular requirement is not connected to values in an obvious way, it is necessary to achieve a goal that is valued: graduation from college.

ACTIVITY 2.2 *Values Sorting*

Use the list that follows to identify your most important values. Limit your selection of values to no more than five by placing an "X" next to the value. Although there may be other values on the list that are important to you, limiting your list to five forces you to identify your most valued values. Feel free to use the "other" option to list a value that is important to you (in your top five) but that is not on the list.

Values List

_____ Good family relationships

_____ Financial security

_____ Job security

_____ A world that is free of discrimination

_____ Creativity

_____ Having a set routine

_____ Time by myself

_____ Community activities

_____ Physical activities

_____ An attractive physical appearance

_____ Variety

_____ Power

_____ Recognition

_____ Prestige

_____ Freedom from stress

Values List

_____ Associating with people I like

_____ Success

_____ Freedom to live where I choose

_____ Leisure time

_____ Fame

_____ Strong religious faith

_____ Good health

_____ Adventure

_____ World peace

_____ A beautiful home

_____ Having children

_____ Autonomy

_____ Helping others

_____ Economic rewards

_____ Other

Now, review your top-five list and try to place them in order of priority from 1 to 5. Write the name of the value next to the appropriate number and then define it for yourself. For example, I may value "economic rewards" and define that as having a job in which I earn $50,000 per year, but someone else may define it as earning no less than $100,000 per year. What matters is how you define it. Take the time to provide your definition. This is an important step; do not skip it

Values Definitions

(1 = most important)

1.

2.

3.

4.

5.

Now, reflect on the goal you identified. How well does the goal you identified connect to your values? If several of your top values connect to your goal, then you are likely to be more motivated to achieve that goal. If not, then you may want to revise your goal so that it is more connected to what is important to you. Finally, try to translate your definition of your most important values into a narrative statement that describes a potential career goal for you to strive toward. For example, if you value autonomy, creativity, economic rewards,

good physical health, and helping others, your narrative statement
could be something like the following:

> I desire a career in which I will work independently, have the
> opportunity to create something to help others, earn a salary of
> at least $75,000 per year, and have enough free time for activities
> such as yoga and rock climbing.

Your statement only needs to incorporate your values; do not worry
about identifying a specific occupation. That can happen later. For
now, it is enough to capture your values, as you define them, in your
narrative statement. This provides a starting place for further reflection and visioning—steps we will discuss later in the book.

Now, look back over what you have written. Are there ways that you
are expressing each of these values in your life currently? If not, what can
you do to change this? If you value living a healthy lifestyle, for example,
what is your diet like? How often do you exercise? Are there changes you
can make so that your life more fully reflects what you value? Identify
any specific change you can make to increase the degree to which you
express your important values in your life. Changes tend to be either to
do more of something or to do less of something. One example could be
something like increasing the number of days you exercise each week
from two to four. Or, you could decide to eat less red meat and more
salads. As you identify specific changes, you are identifying **pathways**
toward achieving your goal, which in this case is increasing the degree to
which you express your important values in your life activities. Pathways
are specific steps you can take in your life to increase the probability of
goal achievement. Try to break your steps into small and specific steps.
For instance, if I decide to increase my exercise time each week but do
not belong to a gym (and want to exercise at a gym), I will first need to
decide which gym I will join. This sounds obvious, but each step must be
divided into smaller steps so that you have clear and specific pathways
toward each goal.

Once you identify the steps you can take toward goal achievement, you
must ask yourself two questions related to each specific step or pathway
you have identified. First, for each step ask yourself how confident you are
that you can successfully complete that step. Rate your confidence on a
scale of 1 (not confident that you can successfully complete the step) to 5
(completely confident that you can successfully complete the step). If you

rate yourself 3 or lower, then you may find it helpful to discuss this with a career advisor or counselor. The focus of the conversation could be what you can do to increase your confidence. You could also examine whether your rating is accurate. That is, do you need to increase your capacity to successfully complete the steps or is your rating more fear based and not a true reflection of your ability to complete the steps you identified? You may also consider whether there are smaller steps you could take that will increase your confidence as you successfully complete them. You might decide, for instance, that while going to the gym four times per week is the eventual goal, starting with two or three times per week is more realistic and a better next step for you to take.

The second question you must ask yourself related to taking the steps you have identified to achieve your goal is whether you are likely to actually take the steps. This question relates to how motivated you are to achieve your goal. You may, for example, be completely confident that you can successfully complete the steps you identified but lack the motivation to do so. Again, rate yourself on a scale of 1 (not motivated at all) to 5 (completely motivated to take the steps you identified). If you rate yourself a 3 or lower, then it is important to consider whether the goal you identified needs to be adjusted so that it is one you are more motivated to achieve. In this case, consider again whether the goal captures qualities you truly value. Look for ways to adjust your goal so that it is more connected to your values. You also may want to discuss with a career advisor or career counselor ways to increase your motivation. It may be helpful to think about whether your beliefs are limiting your motivation. Some beliefs can be self-sabotaging (e.g., "If I take the steps I identified and am successful, others might not approve, so I will not try," or "If I take the steps I identified and it does not work out the way I want it to, then I will be a failure"). False beliefs such as these are artificially self-limiting and fear based. Learning how to counter them with more positive, realistic, and accurate beliefs is important. For example, if you are reluctant to take the steps you identified because you fear "failure," then you may find it helpful to redefine "failure" to focus on "learning." If you take a step and the result is not what you wanted, then you learn important information about yourself and the goal you had identified. When you incorporate this learning into self-understanding and use it to create a new goal, you are, in fact, moving forward in positive and adaptable ways.

When it comes to career decision making, many people think you have to "know" before you can "do." Their thinking is that you must have all the information you need and even a sort of guarantee that a choice will be the "right one" before proceeding with a decision. This is typically an impossible goal to achieve. The fact is that it is not until you actually "do" something that you truly "know" or understand what the choice is like. There is always a knowledge gap when you implement a decision. When you are

> **Tip** Career decisions provide the opportunity to learn more about yourself and your place in the world. Use the learning that comes from every choice to inform your self-awareness and your next choice.

actually living in the decision—when you do it—then you have the information you need to know if the decision was an appropriate one for you. The information you gain by implementing your decision allows you to reflect on the new situation you are in and whether it is wise for you to continue with this decision or use the new information you have acquired to inform you regarding a next choice. Viewing decision making from this perspective is very different than operating from the belief that you are a failure if you make a choice and you subsequently choose to move on to another choice. In fact, taking action and learning from that action is what all "successful" people do! This point is so essential to learn that we will remind you of it throughout this book. For now, trust us, this is a very important shift that most people need to make in how they evaluate their actions.

When you have a goal defined, strategies to achieve your goal clearly clarified, the confidence that you can implement those strategies successfully, and the motivation to do so hope is inevitable. Try it out as an experiment.

ACTIVITY 2.3 *Hope-Action Thinking*

Identify a clear goal that you would like to achieve in the next 2–3 weeks. Make sure the goal is specific, clear (this will help you know if you have actually achieved the goal), and achievable. Write it in the space provided.

Goal:

Pathways: Identify the specific steps you can take to achieve your goal.

Confidence: On a scale from 1 (not confident at all) to 5 (completely confident) rate your level of confidence that you can complete the pathways you identified. If you rate yourself at 4 or 5, then you should proceed to take the steps you identified. If you rate yourself at 3 or below, you should discuss this with a career advisor or career counselor.

Motivation: On a scale of 1 (not motivated) to 5 (highly motivated) rate how motivated you are to complete the pathways you identified. If you rate yourself a 4 or 5, then you should proceed to take the steps you identified. If you rate yourself at 3 or below, you should discuss this with a career advisor or career counselor.

ACTIVITY 2.4 *Hopeful Career State (HCS) Scale*

Hopeful Career State (HCS) Scale was developed to measure your current degree of hopefulness. Follow the directions to learn more about your current situation in relation to your future career. Yoon et al. (2019) found that the higher your score is, the more engaged you will be at work. Greater work engagement connects to greater job satisfaction. In addition, by completing the activities provided in this book you will also increase your hopefulness.

Directions

For each item, rate how true each of the statements is for you using the response scale shown. For example, if the statement is somewhat true for you, put the number 3 in the blank.

**Definitely false: 1   Somewhat false: 2   Somewhat true: 3
Definitely true: 4**

ITEM	SCORE
1. My current work (and/or education) will be helpful for my future career.	_____
2. My current work (and/or education) will enable me to be a better worker in the future.	_____
3. I feel that I am getting closer to better career opportunities.	_____
4. I can think of new employment options because of my current job (and/or program of study).	_____
5. My current job (and/or education) provides resources (e.g., skill development, network, finances) for next steps in my career journey.	_____
6. What I am doing now will help me to build a better career future.	_____
7. What I am doing now is helping me to build skills and experience for the future.	_____
8. What I am doing now is an important step in my career journey.	_____
9. I am hopeful that what I am doing now will help me in my career journey.	_____
Mean score (Total score)	_____

Scoring Instructions

1. Add up your scores for each of the HCS items to determine your total score for the nine items.

2. Divide your total score by nine in order to identify your mean or average score.

3. Record the mean score in the mean score section of the following table. The "Meaning and Action Steps" section of the table helps you understand your current score and explains how this book can help you create hope and develop your career.

Understanding Your Results

YOUR SCORE (X)	MEANING AND ACTION STEPS
X ≤ 2.5	You perceive that your current situation in relation to your career development is not hopeful. You are having difficulties identifying future career options. You may be wondering how your current education and/or work situation connects to future possibilities. There is good news! This book will help you become more hopeful about your situation as you increase your self-understanding and then use this increased understanding to envision future possibilities. Actively implementing action items that you will generate while completing the activities in this book will enhance your hopefulness.
2.5 < X < 3.5	You experience a mix of positives and challenges in your current situation. There is good news for you! This book will help you see the opportunities in your current situation. Specifically, the activities in this book will help you identify ways to turn your current challenges into learning opportunities that you can use to inform your next choice. This approach is key to making good decisions. This book will guide you through the process of increasing your self-understanding, using your increased self-understanding to envision a future you are excited about, and then making plans that will lead you to implementing a decision that will provide you with additional information about yourself and future possibilities.

YOUR SCORE (X)	MEANING AND ACTION STEPS
3.5 ≤ X	You are highly hopeful when you think about your future because you can find numerous opportunities that lead to future possibilities you are excited about. In addition, you feel that your current environment is supportive. By completing this book, you will be able to find and develop concrete strategies and tactics that you can apply in your current and future career. This can lead you to sustain your positive outlook about your situation in relation to your future career.

Summary

We need hope to move forward positively in our lives. Many of us have times in our lives when hope is hard to muster. In these times, planning for our future seems pointless. We feel stuck and unmotivated at these times. There are, however, strategies for generating and sustaining hope in our lives. These strategies are easily learned and can be quickly applied. This chapter reviews those steps. We encourage you to try them out. See the difference they can make for you. Hope fuels planning and our goal in this book is to not only fuel your planning but to help you develop a plan. The steps we will teach you in subsequent chapters, just like the strategies we have addressed in this chapter, are lifelong steps you can take to put your hope into action.

Questions for Reflection and Discussion

1. Identify three goals to achieve in the next 7 days. Identify specific steps to take in order to achieve each of these goals. Review these steps with a mentor, teacher, career advisor, or trusted friend. Ask them if they know of additional steps you could take to achieve each of your goals. Consider all the possibilities. Then, choose specific steps to take. Before you do, however, ask yourself if you are confident that you can complete the steps you identified successfully. Then ask whether you are truly motivated to take the steps. Discuss your responses with a mentor, teacher, career advisor, or trusted friend.

2. Be intentional about saying three positive things to yourself about yourself over the next week. Practice this once in the morning and once in the evening. Pay attention to what this experience is like for you. Consider recording your thoughts in a journal. Note how you feel throughout the week.

References

Averill, J. R., Catlin, G., & Chon, K. K. (1990). *Rules of hope.* Springer-Verlag Publishing. https://doi.org/10.1007/978-1-4613-9674-1

Borgen, W. A., & Amundson, N. E. (1987). The dynamics of unemployment. *Journal of Counseling and Development, 66,* 180–184. https://doi.org/10.1002/j.1556-6676.1987.tb00841.x

Bruininks, P., & Malle, B. F. (2005). Distinguishing hope from optimism and related affective states. *Motivation and Emotion, 29*(4), 327–355. https://doi.org/10.1007/s11031-006-9010-4

Diemer, M. A., & Blustein, D. (2007). Vocational hope and vocational identity: Urban adolescents'career development. *Journal of Career Assessment, 15,* 98–118. https://doi.org/10.1177/1069072706294528

Dufault K., Martocchio B. (1985) Hope: Its spheres and dimensions. *Nursing Clinics of North America, 20,* 379–391

Merriam-Webster Dictionary. (n.d.). *Hope.* http://www.merriam-webster.com/dictionary/hope

DEVELOPING HOPE-ACTION STRENGTHS

3

OBJECTIVES

This chapter focuses on an overview of the hope-action approach to developing your career. After reading and completing activities in this chapter, you will have a beginning understanding of the following:

- The importance of hope in career and educational planning

- How to use self-reflection and self-clarity in educational and career planning

- The difference between objective and subjective career development

- How to use self-clarity to envision future possibilities

CASE EXAMPLE

"My dream started out as an ambition to set foot on each of the seven continents and experience the people, culture, and heartbeat of foreign lands. I began this dream by saving for a trip to Europe at age 15. I spent that summer living with a family in Germany and learned to immerse myself in another world. We learn so much by stepping beyond our comfort level and challenging the mind and spirit by being exposed to new cultures and customs. That first trip became a lifelong obsession that led me to Iceland, India, Russia, the Great Barrier Reef, Fiji, the Maldives and Seychelle Islands, Nepal, Vietnam, Malaysia, and the Serengeti in Africa via overland truck for 11 weeks, just to name a few.

In 1978, after graduating from an all-women's college in Iowa, I began working as a special education and elementary education teacher in Colorado. My desire to impact children's lives through teaching lasted for 20 years and still continues today. I have always maintained a strong connection with family and friends, and, in 1993, I was inspired by my father's dream to climb Mt. Kilimanjaro in Africa. This led to a successful summit of "Kili" on my dad's 61st birthday. He was my inspiration, my friend, and my hero, and 6 years later another climb of one of the world's highest peaks was set in motion. With a successful millennium summit of Mt. Aconcagua, South America's highest peak, the idea to climb the "Seven Summits" was born.

My dream of climbing intensified after my diagnoses of multiple sclerosis in 1999. Waking up with a body that was numb, I feared the worst. I quit my 20-year teaching career, left a 22-year marriage, and felt the panic of needing to complete my chosen task while I was still in control of my physical body. From that point, I saved money when and where I could, and in 2000 used what I had saved to participate in a climb of Mera Peak in Nepal to raise money for a charity. Next, I was off to Russia to climb Europe's highest peak, Mount Elbrus. With my health still strong, I trained on Mexican volcanoes for an attempt of Denali the following spring. With an investment of $10,000 in extreme weather gear, along with a determination that would not stop, I reached the summit of Denali in May of 2006.

Upon returning from Denali, I was told that my persistent back pain was caused by a cyst on a nerve in my spine, which was being pinched between two disks. The cyst developed from a slow leak of spinal fluid, due to a faulty spinal tap by a young medical student when I was first diagnosed with MS in 1999. After back surgery in 2006, and recovery time, followed by training to rebuild my strength, I was ready to move forward again. With ice axe in hand and the desire to complete my dream of setting foot on each continent and climbing the "Seven Summits," I climbed Australia's Mt. Kosciusko in July of 2008 and Mt. Vinson in Antarctica in November 2008. I saved the best for last and set foot on the top of the world, Mt. Everest, on May 23, 2009.

I have been blessed in my life with many gifts, including opportunities to travel and climb. These experiences have enriched my life, and for that I am truly grateful. My biggest reward through all of this has been learning about overcoming fear and limitations and sharing this lesson with others. My desire to impact children's lives has extended to adults and people with disabilities as well. I now give presentations with the message of encouraging others to empower themselves. It is in giving that we receive our greatest gifts.

So my dreams go on, my hopes and health are strong, and I approach my future with a positive outlook. The one vital lesson that I have learned through all of this is not to let your limitations define you and never let go of your dreams. Life is too short not to go for the gusto when you are given the opportunity. I hope that all of your dreams come true as well."

—Lori Schneider
www.empowermentthroughadventure.com/

Lori Schneider, "My Dream." Copyright © by Lori Schneider. Reprinted with permission.

Hope-Action Theory

There are important underlying attitudes and behaviors you must develop to effectively address the career challenges you will experience across your lifetime. Developing these competencies will empower you to cope successfully with the career challenges you experience (Niles, 2014). The Hope-Action Theory provides a competency framework that you can use to address challenges in career and educational planning. Specifically, the Hope-Action Theory competencies are (a) hope, (b) self-reflection, (c) self-clarity, (d) visioning, (e) goal setting/planning, and (f) implementing/adapting.

These competencies draw, in part, on *human agency theory*, developed by well-known Stanford University psychologist Albert Bandura (2001). Human agency relates to understanding who you are and how to develop, implement, and adjust your plans based on new information you acquire about yourself and your situation as a result of actions you take. Hope in action is a concept that also draws on the work of the late Rick Snyder (2002), a psychologist who worked at the University of Kansas. Some people view hope as a passive wishing for a positive outcome. We, however, agree with Snyder. Specifically, we think hope connects to goal-directed actions when you have a clear sense of steps you can take to achieve your goals and when you are motivated to take the steps you identified.

Finally, Douglas Hall, an expert in organizational behavior, highlights the importance of self-clarity and adaptability. Noted for his use of the term the "protean career," Hall (2002) highlights the non-linearity of career development. Moreover, Hall notes that when careers are nonlinear, you need to be vigilant about learning from the experiences you have each day. Collectively, these competencies adapted from the work of Bandura,

Snyder, and Hall provide the foundation for Hope-Action Theory. In this theory, we provide competencies you can develop and use to address career development challenges now and throughout your life. In this chapter, we provide an overview of these competencies. In later chapters, we discuss each competency in more detail.

Hope in Educational and Career Planning

As we discussed in Chapter 1, hope is essential for engaging positively in career planning. Hope is so important that we want to say just a bit more about it. Hope relates to envisioning a meaningful goal and believing that positive outcomes are likely to occur should you take specific actions. Having a sense of hope allows you to consider the possibilities in any situation and propels you to take action (Smith et al., 2014), so much so that without hope people are not likely to take positive action in their lives. In one study, two researchers (Alexander & Onwuegbuzie, 2007) found that people with higher levels of hope were less likely to procrastinate on tasks when compared to those with lower levels of hope. The results of this study remind us of the pervasive importance of having a sense of hope as you manage all aspects of your career development.

In discussing the relationship between hope and goal setting, Snyder (2002) contends that goals necessitating hope must fall in the middle of a probability-of-attainment continuum. This continuum ranges from goals you are certain you will attain to goals you believe are not possible to achieve. If the probability of attaining a goal is either 0% or 100%, then hope is irrelevant for such goals. If goal achievement is impossible you will not be likely to strive toward that goal for very long. If it is guaranteed, then no trying is necessary; therefore, goals must be meaningful and achievable while also challenging.

Having a hopeful attitude enables you to identify one or more action steps you can take to reach your goals (Clarke et al., 2018). When you encounter barriers to goal achievement, you must demonstrate *adaptability* to identify and pursue action steps that address the obstacles you encounter. Adaptability involves the ability to change with change; that is, while you have identified specific goals, you are also open to new information that may influence your goals by either reinforcing them or leading you to develop new ones. Adapting to new information in this way is essential because you are constantly evolving and opportunities—both planned and unplanned—present themselves to you continually. Without hope, however, none of this is possible. You would simply give up when you encounter obstacles (and everyone encounters obstacles to their goals). Researchers have found that people who are low in hope tend to avoid tasks that are necessary to achieve their goals. For example, if a person thinks they are likely to fail a test, they might delay studying for it because they have little hope that studying will lead to a successful outcome (passing the test). A good starting point for considering the importance of hope is to reread the case study provided at the beginning of this chapter and then complete the following activity.

ACTIVITY 3.1 *The Case of Lori*

Refer to the case example at the beginning of the chapter. This is a true story about a real person named Lori Schneider (you can view her website at www.empowermentthroughadventure.com/). Using Lori's story, respond to the following questions:

What obstacles did Lori encounter?

How important was hope for Lori?

How did hope help her achieve her goals?

How might Lori's dream be different if she lacked hope?

In what ways was Lori flexible in identifying new pathways to achieve her goal?

Lori's story illustrates clearly how important hope is in envisioning a dream, setting goals, making plans, and taking action. Lori encountered challenges to achieving her goal, but hope propelled her to keep moving forward. How was she able to do this in the face of significant adversity? In identifying her goal, she first engaged in *self-reflection*, which required her to identify what was important to her (her interests), what she enjoyed (her values), and what skills she possessed and wanted to develop further. Developing answers to questions such as these resulted in *self-clarity*, which she used to engage in *visioning* as she considered future possibilities that were desirable to her. Hope empowered her to consider future possibilities and to identify a specific long-term goal that connected meaningfully to her values, interests, skills, and experiences. Her goal was indeed challenging, but not impossible.

Lori then, initially at the age of 15, made plans for achieving her goal ("to set foot on each of the seven continents and experience the people, culture, and heartbeat of a foreign land"). As she began *implementing* her plan to achieve her goal, Lori was diagnosed with multiple sclerosis. This new information certainly created an obstacle to achieving her goal. This diagnosis required her to evaluate whether her goal was still achievable, and it also required Lori to adjust her plans. Without hope, it would have been perfectly understandable if Lori had chosen at this point to give up on her dream. Yet, she did not give up. Her goal was deeply meaningful to her, so much so that she notes that upon learning her diagnosis she intensified her commitment to her dream. In other words, her diagnosis was a choice point for her. Lori chose to continue taking action to achieve her dream. No doubt, her diagnosis resulted in Lori adjusting her plans as she adapted to her new circumstances. This process propelled her to engage in further self-reflection, resulting in self-clarity as a person with a serious physical challenge, but she continued to follow her dream and adjusted her plans to achieve her goal. Hope was the fuel that propelled her into action.

Lori's story highlights how you can use each of the Hope-Action Theory competencies to manage your career and, frankly, even your life in general. In essence, Lori's story underscores the importance of using hope to engage in self-refection to develop self-clarity. Her hope provides the foundation for future possibilities she envisions and helps her identify a meaningful goal. Because she is hopeful and has a goal, she is able to make specific plans to achieve her goal. She then implements plans of action directed toward achieving her goal while remaining open to revising her plans as they interact with her circumstances. As Lori implements her plans, she will learn more about herself and the world as a result of the actions she has taken. It is, in fact, a never-ending process. The key is paying attention to what you learn about yourself and using this new learning to inform your future course of action.

Developing Hope-Action Theory Competencies

The Hope-Action Theory contains competencies (Figure 3.1) that you can develop and use to engage effectively in career planning. Next, we briefly introduce you to the competencies that are foundational to career decision making.

Self-Reflection

Self-reflection involves the capacity to examine your thoughts, beliefs, behaviors, and circumstances; in essence, it involves paying attention to you and your world. It requires the willingness to consider questions such as the following: What is important to me? What do I enjoy? What skills do I enjoy using? What skills would I like to develop? What opportunities

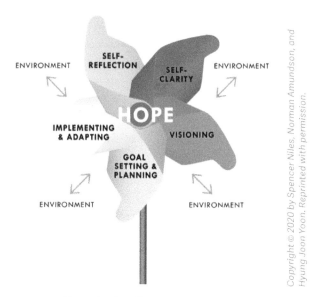

ENVIRONMENT SELF-REFLECTION SELF-CLARITY ENVIRONMENT

HOPE

IMPLEMENTING & ADAPTING VISIONING

GOAL SETTING & PLANNING

ENVIRONMENT ENVIRONMENT

Copyright © 2020 by Spencer Niles, Norman Amundson, and Hyung Joon Yoon. Reprinted with permission.

FIGURE 3.1 *Hope-Action Theory.*

are presented to me in my environment? What sort of lifestyle do I hope to have? How effectively am I using the talents I want to use, engaging in activities that I enjoy, and participating in activities important to me? Am I living the life I want to live? Do I have a vision for my future? The list goes on. Self-reflection involves taking a "time-out" to consider who you are, the life you are living, and the life you hope to live. You should make it a regular practice to engage in this sort of self-reflection. Do this on a weekly basis at first. Writing down your self-reflections will help you to be more systematic and intentional as you consider important questions about yourself and your life.

> **Tip** Be intentional about engaging in systematic self-reflection regarding your thoughts, beliefs, actions, and circumstances. Otherwise, you will miss important opportunities to learn from your experiences.

ACTIVITY 3.2 *Self-Reflections*

Spend 5 minutes in each of the next 5 days considering any of the questions posed. Write down your responses to these questions. After the 5 days, review what you have written.

Consider the following questions:

- What did I learn about myself as a result of this self-reflection activity?

- How does what I wrote about my self-reflections inform me about my future?

As you develop answers to these important questions, you begin the process of developing self-clarity. In this way, self-reflection and self-clarity are linked. Self-reflection involves taking the time to ask the questions. Self-clarity occurs as you do the work to develop answers to the questions about yourself and your circumstances. It is a *process* because the requirement to engage in self-reflection to develop self-clarity is a task that one never completes—it is ongoing and lifelong. Often, you will find it beneficial to engage in self-reflection with a career counselor who can help structure your self-reflection and provide you with important feedback as you consider essential questions about you and your life.

Self-Clarity

With guided and intentional effort, self-clarity emerges. In many ways, the process is similar to developing a photograph. That is, self-reflection is like entering the photographer's darkroom to do the work that results in a clear image (self-clarity). Ancient Greek philosopher Aristotle noted the importance of self-clarity when he emphasized the importance of "knowing thyself" to live life effectively. This advice is essential to managing your career effectively. Everything starts from the foundation of self-awareness. Obviously, developing self-clarity is an ongoing, lifelong process. It is a journey rather than a destination. That said, the clearer you are about who you are, then the easier it is to move forward systematically and intentionally toward a desired destination. If you are not clear about the most basic aspects of your personality—your needs, skills, and so on—then it is likely that you will feel somewhat like a boat adrift at sea, subject to the winds and currents that will direct your course. Developing self-clarity will enable you to be the captain of your ship as opportunities and challenges are presented to you. You will have a foundation of self-understanding that can serve as a lens through which you look at options you are considering.

Unfortunately, many of us prefer to minimize this part of the career development process. Why is that? It seems obvious that it is critical to understand who you are *before* you can decide what career options you will enjoy. So, what might cause us to discount this important step in the process? Perhaps the answer can be found, in part, from the wisdom of Sigmund Freud, who contended that one of the most challenging tasks in life is to learn how to tolerate ambiguity. Humans tend to desire certainty over uncertainty. Denying uncertainty gives many of us a false sense of control over our lives. Unfortunately, this denial often results in just the opposite of control. Denying uncertainty causes us to avoid taking on the challenge of defining who we are and what we want from life. In other words, there is a sort of paradox at work here. Admitting that you are uncertain about your career can often propel you to take the important step of doing the work involved in defining who you are and what you want in life, which is exactly the sort of effort required to take control of your life. Denying uncertainty keeps you stuck in uncertainty, despite any appearance to the contrary.

Trying to make a career decision in the absence of basic self-clarity is similar to taking off on a vacation with no destination and no clear sense about what you hope to experience on your journey. Most people first prefer to identify where they are going and what they hope to experience when they take a vacation. Obviously, making a career decision *after* having developed a basic sense of self-clarity is akin to taking off on a vacation knowing where you want to go, what you hope to experience on your journey, and what you want to do once you arrive at your destination. In both instances, you are likely to have an adventure. One approach—knowing where you want to go—is much more likely to increase the probability that you will experience joy and satisfaction than the other—not knowing where you want to go and what you hope to experience.

Many of us also diminish the importance of putting in the effort toward developing self-clarity because we may interpret such states in a negative way. For example, some people (incorrectly) view being undecided as weak, "wishy-washy," or lazy. Such value judgments ignore the basic fact that everyone (there are no exceptions) has been—at multiple times—undecided about their career goals. It also ignores the fact that being undecided is a necessary step for moving from one option to another. No matter the circumstances, moving from situation A to situation B requires asking whether B is better than A. In other words, you must experience indecision before you can be decided—there is no way around it.

To be clear, you are constantly evolving as a person—no matter what age you are currently. You are constantly experiencing things in your life, and each of these experiences influences who you are and can inform what you want to become. No doubt you know things about yourself and your life today that you did not know 5 years ago. Being open to your ongoing experiences and what they have to teach you influences what you become. The wise person pays attention to this personal evolution and uses it to inform their life choices.

So, remember that you must do the ongoing work to develop self-clarity to make wise career decisions. A basic starting point for doing this work is giving yourself permission to remain uncertain while you figure out what you want to experience next in your career. Do not interpret the necessary step of being uncertain as not making progress in your career development. Do not be fooled into thinking there is nothing happening while you are uncertain. It may, in fact, be the most important work you do in your career decision making—as long as you use your uncertainty wisely. This means engaging intentionally and systematically in self-reflection to develop self-clarity. To develop self-clarity, it is useful to consider objective and subjective dimensions of your career development.

Tip Use both objective and subjective information to inform your career and educational planning.

Using Subjective Information to Develop Self-Clarity

In the area of career development, learning more about oneself is often linked to taking a test. Taking a test can be helpful, and most career centers offer interest inventories, aptitude tests, personality inventories, and so on. Many career assessments focus on helping you identify important self-characteristics—for example, interests and aptitudes—and then comparing your interest and aptitudes to specific occupations. This is an important starting point in gaining self-clarity. It is, however, only a starting point.

The information you acquire from such assessments should propel you to gather more information about occupational options that capture your attention. You can acquire more information through interviewing people who work in occupations that interest you, reading about specific occupations, and/or investing time in exploring occupations through volunteer work, job shadowing, or information interviewing. Whatever sort of information-gathering steps you take, always process the information you acquire through the lens of the information you have developed about your important self-characteristics (that is, your self-clarity). Ask yourself whether you can see yourself spending substantial amounts of time engaged in the work and work environments related to the occupations you are exploring. We discuss all of this in more detail in later chapters.

Information from standardized tests typically is reported in percentile ranks and percentage points; for example, you are provided information about your percentile rank for mathematics ability. Although this information is helpful as a starting point for exploring who you are and how it relates to various occupational options, most of us do not think of ourselves in terms of percentile rankings and percentages. More often, we seek a deeper understanding related to the question of who we are.

These deeper meanings relate to the *subjective experience of career development*, which essentially relates to the process by which people make meaning out of their life experience and translate that meaning into career directions. Both objective and subjective dimensions of self-clarity are important.

One strategy for gaining clarity regarding your subjective career experience comes from Mark Savickas, a vocational psychologist. Savickas (2005) has popularized the view that early life experiences are essential to constructing career plans. Specifically, his career counseling strategies focus on helping people examine early life experiences, often painful, in order to examine how their past connects to their present and informs their future goals. Painful experiences, such as the divorce of one's parents, are key because they often create a yearning for the opposite (e.g., an intact and secure family). Savickas believes we become preoccupied with these early painful experiences, which cause us to turn these into later life occupations. For example, the child who experiences the loss of a loved one may, as an adult, seek to help others cope with loss in their lives. Coping with loss becomes the person's core life theme in this example. The specific occupational title the person assumes, that is, their objective career choice, is less important than whether the job provides an opportunity to be occupied with chances to express the core theme of his or her life (i.e., their subjective career experience). Helping people understand how they can make meaning out of their life experiences and translate that meaning into a career direction is the goal of activities such as the one that Savickas uses to help others identify career goals.

ACTIVITY 3.3 *Preoccupation Exercise*

One way to think more deeply and personally about the way in which you have made meaning out of your life experience is to ask yourself what things you are yearning to experience in your life. In this sense, yearning means more than something you have casually considered every now and again. Rather, in this instance, yearning points to something that is a clear goal that you have consistently considered as important across time. Brainstorm the possibilities by writing them down. If you could experience anything that would be incredibly meaningful in your life, what would it be? Try to come up with at least three possibilities, describing each in detail. Now, consider how what you have identified may be connected to what you experienced in your childhood. Are there any connections? Perhaps the experiences you identified and the things you yearn to experience reveal an opposite experience in your childhood. Do not be too quick to decide there are no connections. In fact, try to identify at least one possible connection (no matter how silly it might seem initially). For example, you may hope to have a connected family of your own. You may already know that you plan to prioritize your family over everything else and you imagine it being the most important thing in the world to you. Upon reflection, you may connect this hope an early life experience in which your family was disconnected. Similarly, over the next few days, reflect on the possibility of this sort of connection between what you yearn to experience in your life and how that may be related to what you experienced early in your life.

1. I yearn to experience the following in my life:

   a.

   b.

   c.

2. One possible connection between what I yearn to experience and my childhood experiences is the following:

Understanding how your life experiences can inform your career direction helps you move forward with intention and purpose. In essence, developing this level of understanding provides the answer to what you will need to do in your life to find meaning in your activities. The task then becomes one of identifying which occupations will provide the greatest opportunity to express yourself in these ways.

An aspect of early life experience that can be a powerful influence in your career development relates to the existence of role models you may have had when you were growing up. Early life role models often are individuals—real or fictional—we seek to pattern our lives after. When you admire someone, you often want to be like that person. For example, Theresa identified Wonder Woman as her early life role model. The strength and integrity of Wonder Woman and her courage to confront challenges in life were some of the qualities that captured Theresa's attention. Theresa encountered multiple early life challenges when her father abandoned her at age 5 and when her mother died from cancer when Theresa was 7. Theresa tried to approach life using the qualities she admired in Wonder Woman. Later, these qualities served her well in her work as a public defender. Connecting these qualities to a potentially satisfying occupation for Theresa meant finding a job that would allow her to manifest the Wonder Woman qualities she prized. Not surprisingly, she was a passionate attorney who cared deeply about helping her clients confront challenges in their lives.

A woman named Verneda identified her elementary school principal as someone she admired when she was young. When asked why, Verneda said the principal tried to help others overcome obstacles they encountered in their lives—that was how he approached his job as a school principal. Later in life, Verneda became a counselor (her objective occupational title) to help others overcome obstacles in life (her subjective meaning she expressed in her work). As they were with Theresa and Verneda, early life role models can be important influences even later in life when you are making important decisions about your career direction.

ACTIVITY 3.4 *Role Model Activity*

Think about your early life experiences and try to identify two or three people you greatly admired. They may have been role models, heroes, or heroines. Perhaps a parent, teacher, coach, or clergy person comes to mind. Your role model can also be a fictional character (e.g., Wonder Woman, Spider Man).

- Once you identify your role model, try to list ways in which you are alike. What similarities do you share? Write them down.

  My role model was (is):

  I am like my role model in these ways:

- Now consider the ways in which you differ from your role model. Write those down.

  I am different from my role model in these ways:

The similarities you identified are important for you to consider in your career decision making. They represent strengths to build on, and they provide an indication of the qualities and competencies you find meaningful and that need to be included in your career activities. They represent core aspects of who you are.

The differences you identified between you and your role model can represent emerging strengths that require further development. They can be labeled as the gap between where you are and where you need to be to grow into your career. You may feel reluctant to engage in these activities because you are not as accomplished in them as you would like to be. However, in many instances, the activities we list when identifying ways in which we differ from our role model can be labeled as developmental skills. These skills, such as public speaking, writing, organizing, and so on, are skills that can be developed and strengthened. Unfortunately, many of us incorrectly conclude that these emerging strengths are "fatal flaws" and indications of why particular career aspirations are unattainable. Although certain skill levels may be unattainable, a significant percentage of activities are of the sort that improvement in performance can be achieved with patience, diligence, and practice.

After you have identified (a) your role model(s), (b) the characteristics you find attractive about your role models, and (c) the ways in which you are similar and different from your role model(s), it is a good idea to translate your list of similarities and differences into goal statements. For example, you may have noted that one of the things you admire about your role model is her skill as a public speaker, but you may feel you do not possess the same ability. You could translate this gap into a goal statement by identifying becoming an effective public speaker as a goal. Then, you could list three to five steps you could take to become a more accomplished public speaker (e.g., taking a speech class, talking to people who you think are effective public speakers and asking them for tips and advice as improving as a speaker, and taking notes of things accomplished speakers do while they speak). In these ways, you can begin to move more intentionally in a direction that will provide a sense of meaning and purpose in your career activity.

ACTIVITY 3.5 *Role Model Goal Statement*

Using similarities and dissimilarities between you and your role model, identify a goal you would like to achieve.

Goal statement:

Three steps I can take to achieve this goal are the following:

1.

2.

3.

Another activity that can help you to learn more about yourself at a deep level is journaling. Keeping a journal provides the opportunity to transfer your reflections, insights, and questions from "head to paper." Not only does this provide you with a document containing important self-information, but it allows you to create a history of your thoughts. After journaling for some time, you can return to read your journal entries, noting any recurring themes. Recurring themes can represent issues or concerns that remain unresolved for you. Sometimes, it is useful to review these themes with a counselor.

Recurring themes can represent wishes placed on hold for a variety of reasons. When dreams persist over time, their existence reflects our inner wisdom about directions for us to head toward. If you think you may have such deferred dreams, you may want to identify one that you could move forward with—even if it is by taking a rather small step. For instance, if you have always wanted to learn how to play the guitar but have never taken a lesson, you might try doing this and seeing how it goes. The point with an activity such as this is not that the activity necessarily represents your future career direction (although it may). The point is that, in moving forward with a deferred dream, you will learn something about yourself and how you make decisions. You may learn to trust your instincts more than you had before. You may learn the importance of intuition in the decision-making process. You may learn to pay greater attention to intuition in your subsequent decisions. You will also very likely learn something about the activity you pursue and whether it is appropriate for you. You will learn more about yourself.

Life provides countless learning experiences across the life span. You will continue to grow and develop. New interests may emerge, untapped interests may be tapped, you may learn new skills, and certain values may become either less or more important as your career unfolds and as you take on new roles in life. When you pay attention to who you are and who you are becoming, you acquire important information that will help you manage your career flow experiences.

Using Self-Clarity to Envision Future Possibilities

Paying attention to who you are and who you are becoming requires vigilance relative developing self-clarity. As you are constantly evolving, so the task of understanding your self is also constant. Assessing your values, interest, skills, etc., is an important lifelong task. Developing self-clarity is important because you use self-clarity to create a vision of your future possibilities.

Visioning

Visioning involves brainstorming future possibilities for your career and identifying your desired future outcomes. Brainstorming focuses on quantity rather than quality. In this instance, quantity relates to using your self-clarity to develop as many career options as possible. For example, given what you know to be true about yourself and your circumstances, what career options come to mind? Make the list as expansive as possible. Enlist the help of a friend and/or a career coach as you identify future possibilities. Be creative and have fun!

ACTIVITY 3.6 *Visioning*

- Based on what I know about myself, I can envision the following possibilities:

- Once you have generated a lengthy list of possibilities, identify which ones seem to make the most sense—based on your self-clarity—to learn more about and to consider further.

- From the list, the following options make the most sense to learn more about:

You may need to acquire additional information through reading, talking with others engaged in occupations of interest, and so on, but once you have gathered additional information, return to what you know about yourself and your circumstances. Always consider possible options in light of your self-clarity. All the information you have acquired will guide you as you engage in *goal setting and planning*, which are discussed in detail in a later chapter.

Once you have identified your goals and developed plans for achieving them, you are ready to implement your plans. Implementing means taking actions that are in line with your plans and goals. For example, if you have engaged in self-reflection to develop self-clarity regarding possible academic majors—and then used your self-clarity to envision possible majors and related occupations, established goals, and identified plans to enroll in a specific major—your next step is to enroll in that major (implementing). As you begin taking courses in that academic major, you will monitor and evaluate whether the major connects as closely to your goals, values, interest, and skills as you hoped it would. If it does, then you simply proceed, pursuing your identified goal. If it does not seem to fit as well as you had hoped, then you will need to adapt your plans.

> **Tip** Develop plans to achieve your goals and revise your plans as necessary.

Summary

Although there are specific strategies you will need to use to manage different dimensions of your career, the model introduced briefly in this chapter provides the foundation for addressing all aspects of your career development. Engaging in the activities presented in this chapter will help you develop Hope-Action Theory competencies. As the process becomes more natural, you will be able to incorporate it more readily into your educational and career planning. When you implement career goals guided by self-clarity emerging from systematic and intentional self-reflection, you are able to make career decisions in a positive, confident, and hopeful manner.

Questions for Reflection and Discussion

1. Complete the self-assessment activity at the end of this chapter. Score your results and identify the areas you need to develop. Take at least one step to develop the career flow competencies that need strengthening.

2. What can you learn from Lori Schneider's dream?

3. Apply each step of the model presented in this chapter to Lori's dream.

4. How hopeful are you about your future?

5. What could you do to strengthen your sense of hope for the future?

6. How often do you engage in self-reflection in the ways we discussed in this chapter?

7. Try to set aside specific times this week for engaging in self-reflection about what is important to you, what you enjoy doing, and what you hope for in your future.

References

Alexander, E. S., & Onwuegbuzie, A. J. (2007). Academic procrastination and the role of hope as a coping strategy. *Personality and Individual Differences, 42*(7), 1301–1310. https://doi.org/10.1016/j.paid.2006.10.008

Bandura, A. (2001). Social cognitive theory: An agentic perspective. *Annual Review of Psychology, 52*, 1–26. https://doi.org/10.1146/annurev.psych.52.1.1

Clarke, A., Amundson, N. E., Niles, S. G., & Yoon, H. J. (2018). Hope: An agent of change for internationally educated professionals. *Journal of Employment Counseling, 55*(4), 155–165. https://doi.org/10.1002/joec.12095

Hall, D. T. (2002). *Careers in and out of organizations*. SAGE.

Niles, S. G. (2011). Career flow: A hope-centered model of career development. *Journal of Employment Counseling, 48*, 173–175. *https://doi.org/10.1002/j.2161-1920.2011.tb01107.x*

Niles, S. G. (2014). Using an action-oriented hope-centered model of career development. *Journal of Asia Pacific Counseling, 4*(1), 1–13. https://doi.org/10.1002/j.2161-1920.2011.tb01107.x

Savickas, M. L. (2005). The theory and practice of career construction. In S. D. Brown & R. W. Lent (Eds.), *Career development and counseling: Putting theory and research to work* (pp. 42–70). Wiley.

Smith, B. A., Mills, L., Amundson, N., Niles, S., Yoon, H. J. & In, H. (2014). What helps and hinders post-secondary students who maintain high levels of hope despite experiencing significant barriers. *Canadian Journal of Career Development, 13*(2), 59–74.

Snyder, C. R. (2002). Target article: Hope theory: Rainbows in the mind. *Psychological Inquiry, 13*(4), 249–275. https://doi.org/10.1207/S15327965PLI1304_01

Additional Resources

Go to Lori Schneider's website to learn more about the importance of hope in goal achievement: www.empowermentthroughadventure.com/

Visit this site to learn more about hope and happiness and how important it is in how you live your life: www.authentichappiness.sas.upenn.edu/Default.aspx

Hope-Action Inventory

The Hope-Action Inventory (HAI) (Niles et al., 2011) allows you to assess the level of your hope-action competencies. It can be taken by going to www.hopecenteredcareer.com/hai. A code will be available via Cognella Active Learning or can be purchased on the website. While examining your hope-action competencies, practice and/or reflect on these points regularly.

Strategies for Developing Hope-Action Competencies

1. Hope

   - Engage daily in positive self-talk (e.g., "I can take control of my life," "My future will be bright," "I deserve to be loved").

   - Identify the positive aspects of your current circumstances in life.

   - Review Lori Schneider's website and reflect on how she managed to stay hopeful despite the challenges in her life.

   - Identify one famous person whom you admire and then read what you can about them on the internet. What challenges did the person overcome? How was the person able to maintain a sense of hope?

2. Self-reflection

   - Identify your happiest moments and describe in writing what you were doing in those moments.

   - Reflect on those things in life about which you are passionate.

   - Identify activities and experiences that give you joy.

   - Consider your family, friends, and current or former coworkers and think about how you tend to interact with them. What do you like about how you interact with them? What would you like to change about your interactions?

3. Self-clarity

   - List three activities you really enjoy participating in.

   - List three skills you enjoy using the most.

- List three things that are most important to you.

- Write a sentence, paragraph, or one page describing yourself, integrating important points about your values, skills, interests, life roles, motives, and personality.

4. Visioning

- Consider which life roles are most important to you and what you would like to accomplish in each of those roles in the next 5 years.

- If you won the lottery tomorrow, what would want to be doing 5 years from now?

- If you won the lottery tomorrow and could do anything *other than what you identified thus far*, what would you want to be doing 5 years from now?

- Revisit your desired future scenarios regularly (at least once per week).

5. Goal setting and planning

- Set specific and measurable goals for the next several years according to your important values and vision.

- Brainstorm and make a list of steps you can take to reach your goals.

- Develop weekly plans that reflect your long-term goals.

- Identify one thing you hope to accomplish today and incorporate it into a to-do list for the day.

6. Implementing and adapting

- Identify one action step you can take to implement your plan to achieve one of your goals.

- Commit yourself promptly to your plans once you think they have been clearly articulated.

- Monitor your progress toward your goals and your plan on a weekly and/or daily basis.

- When necessary, adjust your plans or actions when you encounter substantial barriers or better opportunities.

Section I provides the foundation for understanding the centrality of hope in career development. We offer an assessment to help you identify your current level of hopefulness. Then, we introduce you to the theory developed by Niles, Amundson and Yoon (2010) that describes competencies you can use across your lifetime to guide you in your career decision-making as you strengthen your sense of hopefulness for your next career move. Finally, we focus on what you can do to create hope in your life. We also present important activities to help you achieve a greater level of hopefulness. These activities address self-awareness that will become a prominent aspect of your work in the next sections as you develop possibilities for your future based on what you are learning about yourself.

In Section II, we dig more deeply into self-reflection and self-clarity activities. We deconstruct the essential elements of these two factors and offer specific exercises you can use to enhance self-reflection and develop self-clarity. This work is crucial for developing the level of awareness you need for managing your career effectively. Everything else you do in your planning will be grounded in developing a clear sense of who you are and who you hope to become. This understanding should drive the possibilities and future vision you create for yourself. So, do not move too quickly through this section. The activities we provide will pay major dividends as you develop a vision for your future, engage in job searching, and continue reflecting on who you are, who you are becoming, and who you hope to be.

SELF-REFLECTION AND SELF-CLARITY

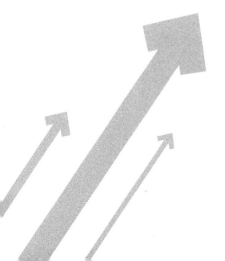

4 PURSUING YOUR INTERESTS (PASSIONS)

OBJECTIVES

This chapter focuses on the process of attaining greater self-clarity by focusing on interests. After reading and completing activities in this chapter, you will be able to do the following:

- Identify your full range of interests—both what you enjoy and what you don't—and analyze the patterns imbedded in these interests

- Use the theory of John Holland to identify your interests

- Find matching occupational options according to your Holland codes

CASE EXAMPLE

Santosh's family moved to America from India about seven years ago. He is the eldest of five children and is part of a large extended family. His father is an engineer and his mother has training as a librarian but stays at home with the younger children. Santosh did well in school and was very good with computers. His father encouraged him to pursue this interest, and he has been working in the import/export business in a computer support position. He lost this job during the recent health crisis but was fortunate and soon found another position in an Internet company that focuses on internal communication within companies.

While Santosh is currently doing well in his work, he is not sure that this is the field that he ultimately wants to pursue. He is competent at handling the technical part of computers, but only really gets excited when he is teaching others. Informally, he works with two of his younger nieces and loves teaching them how to use the computer. His friends also rely on him for computer assistance and he loves showing them what he has learned.

Santosh is fully engaged when he is teaching others how to use computers. He is patient, thoughtful, and encouraging, and he seems to be able to work well with people of all ages. A major problem, however, is the fact that his father does not want him wasting his time in the educational field as a teacher. His father feels that teaching does not pay well and ultimately many teachers end up being burned out by the end of their career. His mother is more open-minded about career possibilities, but she goes along with her husband's wishes.

Santosh does not want to go against his father's wishes, but also believes that he should be responsible for his own career choices. He doesn't want to find himself at the end of his career regretting the fact that he never took the opportunity to train others.

n this case example Santosh seems to be aware of his interests. However, he also must deal with pressure from his father. This is a common dilemma for many people, and it can be worthwhile to think about different ways of handling a situation where there are differences of opinion within families.

Identifying and Analyzing a Full Range of Interests

This workbook presents the argument that the pursuit of one's interests (passions) is often the best option (Tamny, 2018). People who are able to pursue their passions while at work are more engaged and usually more successful. Dr. Robert Cooper (2001) makes the following observation:

> Research on more than 400,000 Americans over the past 40 years indicates that pursuing your passions—even in small doses, here and there each day—helps you make the most of your current capabilities and encourages you to develop new ones. It can also help keep you feeling younger throughout your life! (p. 89)

Cooper (2001) goes on to describe a research study that focuses on how much money people make when they pursue their passions. In this classic study the researcher interviewed 1,500 business school students who were classified into two groups. One group (1,245) seemed to be at college mainly for the money. The other smaller group (255) was intent on using their degree to do something they cared deeply about. These students were followed up 20 years later and the researcher discovered that 101 of them had attained millionaire status. The interesting part was that all but one of the millionaires came from the 255 students who were pursuing their education so that they could advance their passion.

This discussion is meant to open you to the idea that discovering your passions is an important element in the career development process. But what if you have more than one passion? How does one identify the full range of passions that one can draw from? A starting point is a simple exercise where you take a blank piece of paper and just start writing down all the things you enjoy doing. Don't restrict yourself to work or education; think broadly about your life and what brings you joy. You might be someone who likes going for walks, or going to the cinema, or cooking special dinners for friends. Whatever you enjoy, write it down in the space provided.

ACTIVITY 4.1 *Things I Enjoy Doing*

These are the things I enjoy doing during leisure, work and family time:

- _____

- _____

- _____

- _____

Now that you have your list, look over it and add some other things that you might enjoy doing but haven't yet had the opportunity to try. Use a different color pen to differentiate these other items from what you have on your original list.

If you find yourself with very few items on the page, think back to what you enjoyed a few years ago. Try to make the list as complete as possible.

Now that you have these interests listed, do an analysis of your top five interests by answering the following questions for all five:

1. I enjoyed _____.

- When was the last time I actually did this activity?

  _____

- Was the activity something I did alone or with others?

  _____

- How much planning was necessary to do this activity?

  _____

- What is it that I get from doing this activity (i.e., how does it impact me physically, mentally, emotionally and spiritually)?

  _____

- What would I need to do to make more room in my life for this activity?

  _____

2. I enjoyed _____.

- When was the last time I actually did this activity?

  _____

- Was the activity something I did alone or with others?

  _____

- How much planning was necessary to do this activity?

  _____

- What is it that I get from doing this activity (i.e., how does it impact me physically, mentally, emotionally and spiritually)?

  _____

- What would I need to do to make more room in my life for this activity?

  _____

3. I enjoyed _____.

  - When was the last time I actually did this activity?

    _____

  - Was the activity something I did alone or with others?

    _____

  - How much planning was necessary to do this activity?

    _____

  - What is it that I get from doing this activity (i.e., how does it impact me physically, mentally, emotionally and spiritually)?

    _____

  - What would I need to do to make more room in my life for this activity?

    _____

4. I enjoyed _____.

  - When was the last time I actually did this activity?

    _____

- Was the activity something I did alone or with others?

  _____

- How much planning was necessary to do this activity?

  _____

- What is it that I get from doing this activity (i.e., how does it impact me physically, mentally, emotionally and spiritually)?

  _____

- What would I need to do to make more room in my life for this activity?

  _____

5. I enjoyed _____.

- When was the last time I actually did this activity?

  _____

- Was the activity something I did alone or with others?

  _____

- How much planning was necessary to do this activity?

  _____

- What is it that I get from doing this activity (i.e., how does it impact me physically, mentally, emotionally and spiritually)?

  _____

- What would I need to do to make more room in my life for this activity?

  _____

Analysis: Looking at your top five activities and also other activities on your list, what themes can you draw out? For example, you might see that you enjoy being in situations where there is some personal challenge that must be overcome. Or perhaps there is some need to have an outlet for getting away from the stresses of everyday life. Whatever the pattern, think broadly about the underlying dynamics that make the activity satisfying to you. Note: It can be very helpful to have input from others in doing this analysis. If you are in a group context you might want to break into small groups for discussion and analysis.

_____

_____

_____

_____

_____

_____

Application: How will you be able to incorporate some of the patterns that you have identified with the career/life goals that you are pursuing? Are these patterns reflected in the educational and work life choices that you are making?

_____

_____

_____

_____

_____

The previous exercise focuses on things you enjoy doing, but what happens if you take the opposite approach? What are some things that you don't enjoy doing? Take a moment to create a list of some things that definitely don't fit into your interest list.

_____

_____

_____

_____

_____

ACTIVITY 4.2 *Things I Don't Enjoy Doing*

These are the things I don't enjoy doing during leisure, work and family time:

- _____

- _____

Take some of these activities and flip them around, looking at the reverse perspective. For example, say you definitely don't enjoy opening packages and putting things together. The frustrating part might be reading the manuals and trying to make everything fit. If you look at this from the flip side, you might say that you are more of a "big picture" kind of person and don't really like focusing on the details. Or, it might just be the manuals that you don't like reading. Perhaps you learn better through experiential learning.

Take five of the activities that you have listed and determine the flip side. What ideas come to you when you start from this perspective?

The Flip Side

1. I don't enjoy _____

The flip side of this is

_____

_____

_____

_____

_____

2. I don't enjoy _____.

The flip side of this is

_____

_____

_____

_____

3. I don't enjoy _____.

The flip side of this is

_____

_____

_____

_____

4. I don't enjoy _____

   The flip side of this is

_____

_____

_____

_____

_____

5. I don't enjoy _____

   The flip side of this is

_____

_____

_____

_____

Analysis: Looking at these five activities and also other activities on your list, what themes can you draw out? Look at the trends and patterns in your responses. Note: As before, it can be very helpful to have input from others in doing this analysis. If you are in a group context you might want to break into small groups for discussion and analysis.

_____

_____

_____

_____

_____

_____

Application: How will you be able to incorporate some of the patterns that you have identified with the career/life goals that you are pursuing? Are these patterns reflected in the educational and work life choices that you are making?

_____

_____

_____

_____

_____

_____

Viewing Interests Through the John Holland Lens

Dr. John Holland (1994), a well-known career development specialist, has developed a widely used classification system that can be helpful in analyzing people and work environments. With this approach there is the assumption that there are six different types of interests/personality that influence career decision making. These six types can be described as follows:

Realistic (R)

People with this type enjoy working with tools, objects, machines, or animals, and through this process they acquire manual, mechanical, agricultural, and/or electrical skills. They are practical, hands-on people who focus their energy on making things work. The occupations in this area focus on building things or making repairs.

Tip By examining your interests in a more in-depth manner you will be able to derive some of the underlying patterns that help to determine your overall satisfaction level. The challenge is to systematically incorporate the patterns into all of your career and life activity.

Investigative (I)

People with this type enjoy being involved in the biological and physical sciences and develop mathematical and scientific skills. They are curious, studious, and independent. The occupations in this area focus on the scientific and medical fields.

Artistic (A)

People with this type enjoy being involved in creative activities where there is variety and less routine. They develop skills in language, art, music, and drama and tend to be innovative and open-minded. The occupations in this area focus on fields where there is some flexibility and the opportunity to apply their creative talents.

Social (S)

People with this type seek activities where they can interact with others through teaching and offering emotional support and guidance. They are helpful and friendly and develop good communications skills. The occupations in this area focus on fields such as social work, nursing, teaching, and counseling.

Enterprising (E)

People with this type enjoy leading or influencing other people. They have developed good communication skills and can be quite persuasive. They also are ambitious, outgoing, energetic, and self-confident. The occupations in this area involve sales and management and they also find themselves drawn to self-employment.

Conventional (C)

People with this type are focused on organizing information in a clear and precise manner and to do this they use their organizational and clerical skills. In carrying out these tasks they are responsible, dependable, and detail oriented.

ACTIVITY 4.3 *Using the John Holland System*

As you think about yourself and your interests/personality, which of these types seems the best fit for you? Holland suggests that up to three of these types need to be considered. Rank order your top three choices. While you can determine your codes by understanding each of the personality types, taking an assessment could be helpful. O*NET Interest Profiler (www.mynextmove.org/explore/ip) is a free assessment tool that allows you to find your codes and matching occupational titles. Note: As an alternative, you may want to use John Holland's Self-Directed Search instrument (www.self-directed-search.com/) to help you with this analysis.

1. _____

2. _____

3. _____

As an example, suppose that social was your first choice but you also felt some connection with enterprising and artistic; then your Holland code would be SEA. With this profile you might want to consider working in fields such as social work, counseling, human resource management, special education, being a community organizer, and so on. Once you have your code you can look for programs of study that match your interests using the Educational Opportunities Finder (Rosen et al., 1999). You can also find work possibilities by using resources such as the Occupations Finder (Holland, 1994), the Dictionary of Holland Occupational Titles (Gottfredson & Holland, 1996), or the O*NET database (www.onetcenter.org/), sponsored by the U.S. Department of Labor.

Among these resources, the most easily accessible and comprehensive one is the O*NET database. To find matching occupational titles using your Holland codes, visit www.onetonline.org/explore/interests and click on your primary code (e.g., realistic). Then, the next screen will allow you to enter the second and third codes. For example, if your Holland codes are SEA, select social, enterprising, and artistic from each of the drop-down menus, respectively. You may choose to enter one or two codes only in order to expand your search. You will be able to review suggested occupational titles that match with your Holland codes.

List up to five that you would like to explore further as your potential career options:

1. _____

2. _____

3. _____

4. _____

5. _____

To expand the range of possibilities you might want to mix the codes a little (the O*NET page gives you results with all potential combinations). For example, you might want to consider the following: SEA, SAE, ASE, AES, ESA, EAS. By using this broader range you increase the number of occupational or educational options. Now it's your turn; list at least five addition career options that fit with a more expanded code selection:

1. _____

2. _____

3. _____

4. _____

5. _____

Make a note of any career options that appear interesting and that you would like to explore further.

Santosh, the case example in this chapter, can't seem to come to terms with the idea of teaching and decides to do some informational interviewing with a family friend (a teacher). He discovers that even though teachers are now using more online resources in their teaching, there are still some significant disadvantages. He decides that maybe becoming a school teacher isn't the best choice for him.

It is nice to get a regular paycheck, even though the job itself isn't that interesting. Most of his time is spent in a reactive mode solving various computer problems. He wonders whether maybe he was expecting too much from working life—after all, he has a permanent job, he is getting good money, and he also enjoys the people he is working with. However, he still clings to some faint hope that there might be some way of finding work that is more in line with his career passion.

There are many people who have walked the same road as Santosh. They have found work that might meet one of their interests but remain unfilled in the work that they are doing. In this workbook we are suggesting that perhaps there is something more that people should strive toward. Let's see how Santosh resolves this dilemma.

After about six months on the job, Santosh finds that he is becoming increasingly frustrated. He sees the same mistakes being made over and over again. After a discussion with his supervisor he decides to offer some preliminary training groups for people in his company. The first group was poorly attended, but the results were good and after a couple of months the word was spreading that this training was really worthwhile. Santosh thoroughly enjoys doing the training and soon finds that his job satisfaction has increased immeasurably. He loves teaching and showing people how to get the most out of their computers. Finally, his career passion is starting to align with the work he is doing.

Even though Santosh is working in the computer field, he is now starting to also engage his other interest in teaching (which coincides with career flow). By combining these two interests he has dramatically improved his chances of deriving long-term satisfaction with his work. While teaching computers in an educational setting was one option, it was not the only way in which these two interests could be combined. It is important to sometimes "think outside the box" when planning one's career.

Obviously when making the leap from interests to options it is helpful to start by working in career areas where there are good opportunities to use most of your interests. However, the workplace is very diverse, and it is important in this diversity to have a good sense of what interests you would like to apply. Career development is not just about landing in the right field; it is an ongoing process that includes many career decisions throughout life.

Viewing Interests as Part of a Larger Centric Wheel Framework

There is little doubt that interests play an important role in furthering career development. But is there more that needs to be considered? Is it enough to just be interested in pursuing a certain field? A broader framework such as the centric wheel needs to be utilized. The centric wheel highlights both internal (skills, interests, values, personal style) and external (significant others, learning experiences, work/life experiences, career opportunities) factors (Amundson, 1989; Amundson & Poehnell, 2003).

Interests represent one piece of the wheel and point toward certain career alternatives. But, there also are many other factors that need to be taken into account.

The dotted line on the figure is done purposefully to illustrate that the factors can vary in size and importance. In the case study, for example, it is clear that while interests were important for Santosh, the opinions of his father (a significant other) were of even greater importance. Thus,

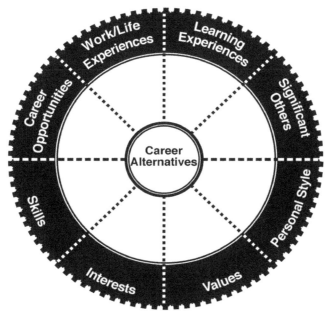

Copyright © 2008 by Ergon Communications.

FIGURE 4.1 *Career wheel.*

for Santosh, the significant other part of the wheel might be two or three times larger than any of the other pieces.

The upcoming chapters will reference various segments of the wheel as we broaden the level of inquiry. This is a holistic model in the sense that one only gets to the center point by considering all the different factors. In broadening the exploration there is the opportunity to discover whether there is a convergence of ideas through the various segments.

Summary

This chapter introduced two different ways of examining interests. As a starting point there was the focus on in-depth exploration of things you enjoy doing and things that you don't enjoy doing (flipping them around to attain a new perspective). This exploration led to the identification of personal patterns and to the consideration of how these patterns might be applied in other situations. The second level of analysis focused on the more traditional John Holland matching approach where six different perspectives are used to determine one's career code. It is then possible to match one's Holland code with occupational and educational options.

Questions for Reflection and Discussion

1. Can you think of a situation in your own life or in the life of someone you know where following one's interest conflicts with the wishes of others? Describe the situation and discuss some of the strategies for dealing with these kinds of conflicts.

2. When Santosh was resolving his situation he had to "think outside the box." Have you been in situations where you had to be creative to ensure that your needs were being fulfilled? Describe the situation and discuss some of the dynamics.

3. When you think of interests as part of the wheel, how big do you think it is in relation to the other components (i.e., same as the others, larger, smaller)? What accounts for the choice that you are making and how might this impact your future career/life choices?

References

Amundson, N. E. (1989). A model of individual career counseling. *Journal of Employment Counseling, 26*(3), 132–138. https://doi.org/10.1002/j.2161-1920.1989.tb00943.x

Amundson, N. E. & Poehnell, G. (2003). *Career pathways* (3rd ed.). Ergon Communications.

Cooper, R. K. (2001). *The other 90%: How to unlock your vast untapped potential for leadership and life.* Three Rivers Press.

Gottfredson, L. S. & Holland, J. L. (1996). *The dictionary of Holland occupational codes.* Psychological Assessment Resources.

Holland, J. L. (1994). *The occupations finder.* Psychological Assessment Resources.

Rosen, D., Holmberg, K. & Holland, J. L. (1999). *The educational opportunities finder.* Psychological Assessment Resources.

Tamny, J. (2018). *The end of work: Why your passions can become your job.* Regnery.

5 MAPPING YOUR SKILLS: THOSE YOU HAVE AND THOSE YOU NEED

OBJECTIVES

This chapter focuses on the role of skills and competencies in career development. After reading and completing activities in this chapter, you will be able to do the following:

- Map your accomplishments and transferable skills
- Benchmark your skills/competencies against others who are successful in work that interests you
- Conduct a gap analysis
- Implement strategies to compensate for skill deficits
- Prioritize skills/competencies to showcase them

CASE EXAMPLE

Sandeep was so excited to be graduating next term. Originally from India, Sandeep has been an international student for 6 years and, for his second-to-final term, had secured a wonderful internship in the human resources (HR) department of a large nonprofit organization. He especially enjoyed working as part of a friendly team; they had quickly became like family for him.

Sandeep's parents and three of his siblings had booked flights to come out for his graduation. They were looking forward to traveling together throughout the United States and Canada after the term ended and had planned several big celebrations with extended family members in various cities across the continent.

The COVID-19 pandemic changed all of that, very suddenly! Although Sandeep's internship continued, he was expected to work from home. For some of his teammates, this wasn't much of a hardship—in Zoom meetings, he could see their beautiful, spacious homes. However, Sandeep was sharing a dorm room at the university where all classes had been rescheduled to be online. His roommate was laid-off from his part-time job in a restaurant, so was home all day, too. For over a month, they had been "self-isolating"—keeping a 2-meter distance from others and only shopping for essential groceries once per week.

Sandeep found himself with lots of time on his hands to reflect. He made a conscious choice to make the most of this time when the whole world quieted down. In some ways, it was exciting to have all his plans for the next several months swept away. Graduation was now going to be virtual, and nonessential international travel wasn't permitted, so Sandeep's family wouldn't be coming for graduation or traveling together afterward. The final term's classes would be online. Sandeep decided to view this time as a pregraduation gift to reflect on what skills he'd developed through his courses and internship and what skill gaps still needed to be filled. He recognized that work opportunities would be different than he'd anticipated when he graduated and wanted to be well-prepared when the economy started to come back to life.

n some ways, Sandeep's experience is similar to so many other students as they prepare to graduate and transition into the workforce. He's grateful to be in a program that offers some work experience and appreciates what he's learning through his internship. As an international student, however, he's had less paid work experience than many of his local peers. Through his studies and internship in HR, Sandeep knows that employers make hiring decisions based on prior work. He recognizes, however, that, lack of *paid* work experience does not mean lack of *relevant* experience for a job.

The key is to identify measurable accomplishments and transferable skills/competencies that will convince potential employers that you have exactly what they are looking for. Achieving greater self-clarity about your skills will, in turn, increase your optimism and hopefulness. Hope is at the center of the Hope-Action Theory, and it's important to realize that evidence of skills can be found in school, internships, and many other activities—not just paid work.

In this chapter, step-by-step instructions are provided for mining your rich life experiences, translating those experiences into language employers will recognize, and making a clear and compelling argument that your experiences are equivalent to, or better than, the paid work experience they request. Of course, the information in this chapter is also relevant to those who already have lots of work experience and will also assist with identifying and filling gaps between the skills and competencies you currently have and those you'll need to grow your career. Throughout our careers, we all need the ability to translate diverse work and life experiences into language that a recruiter, human resource professional, or hiring manager will understand. This chapter will equip you to recognize and communicate transferable skills/competencies, benchmark your skills/competencies against people who are successful in the work that you are interested in, develop strategies to build the skills you need and/or compensate for skill deficits, and organize complex information into concrete evidence that proves you have what it takes to successfully transition into work that interests you.

Mapping Accomplishments and Transferable Skills

An important starting place is to generate a list of accomplishments. This is different from a list of duties, responsibilities, or course requirements. Rather, it documents *outcomes* of your activities, demonstrating your achievements from a variety of life arenas.

Kris Magnusson (2001), a Canadian counselor-educator, developed a framework that may help you begin your accomplishment profiling: the 5 Ps—pride, passion, purpose, performance, and poise. In order to find work you can thrive in, it's essential to recognize your special talents and effectively articulate them to others. Systematically collecting evidence of your skills and competencies—for example, in a career portfolio that organizes samples of your accomplishments at school and/or work—is an important ongoing activity. The following exercise will help you get started.

ACTIVITY 5.1 *Accomplishment Profile*

The following eight steps will help you profile your accomplishments. Use the space provided for your reflections.

1. Begin by reflecting on moments in life when you've been particularly proud. *Sandeep wrote, "It was very exciting to be accepted in
   the business school of a prestigious international university."*

   _____

   _____

   _____

2. Recognize your contribution to those proud moments. *Sandeep
   wrote, "At first I was nervous about applying for international
   universities. However, I spoke to my mentor who helped me see
   what I could contribute and what I could learn through this. I then
   consulted with a coach to help with my applications. I watched
   North American television to improve my understanding of local
   language and to become more familiar with different accents. I
   arranged some volunteer work to strengthen my application and
   also got some very strong letters of reference from previous teachers. I connected with relatives attending the universities that I was
   applying to, to get a better understanding of what would make my
   applications strong."*

   _____

   _____

   _____

   _____

3. Think of your proud moment as a story. For each story, brainstorm
   a brief title and create a list of your personal contributions, that
   is, tasks you completed that resulted in the accomplishment.
   *Sandeep called his story "Becoming an International Student" and
   listed a few tasks: consult with mentor, access coaching, language*

immersion, volunteer work, reference letters, and connect with relatives for tips.

_____

_____

_____

_____

4. Summarize a significant accomplishment or outcome for each proud moment. *Sandeep wrote, "I was offered scholarships to attend three prestigious universities."*

_____

_____

_____

_____

5. Take a holistic, "big picture" look at your accomplishments. Identify recurring patterns or themes; these likely represent something you are passionate about. *As Sandeep reflected on other accomplishments, he noticed that he always consulted with others and addressed his skill gaps quickly such as arranging for reference letters and volunteer experience and increasing his comfort with the local accent and idioms.*

_____

_____

_____

_____

6. Reflect on your passions as revealed by your life accomplishments. Identify how best to put your passions into action; this will help to clarify your purpose or career goals. *Sandeep wrote, "I am passionate about making people's lives better, especially when they are at work. I want to work in an organization that is doing something important and meaningful, and that treats people well."*

_____

_____

_____

_____

7. The next step in the 5 Ps model is performance—finding a purposeful outlet for your passions. List places where you used your skills or demonstrated your competencies; examples might include at a specific job, during a volunteer activity, or in a sport. *Sandeep listed his internship experience.*

_____

_____

_____

_____

8. Finally, poise comes from practice. Many of the highlights of your life and career—your accomplishments—likely occurred after you practiced a skill to the point of achieving poise. Record those accomplishments in rich detail to reflect on and to share with others who have the potential to impact your career. *Sandeep wrote, "I am confident connecting people to other people or to the resources they need to be successful at work. I earned 90% on three of my recent school projects that involved developing innovative HR programs and services. My internship supervisor told me* *that connecting her to a local community agency has opened up access to a new source of volunteers to support their programs."*

_____

_____

_____

_____

_____

As you share such accomplishments—on your resume, in a cover letter, through a career portfolio, at a networking event, in a job interview, or online (e.g., LinkedIn, Instagram)—your enthusiasm and energy (i.e., your passion) and your skills/competencies and knowledge (i.e., your performance and poise) will shine through. These naturally exuberant moments of sharing will attract others' attention; you won't need to obnoxiously brag. Rather, as you are genuinely focused on fulfilling your life's purpose, your accomplishments will speak for themselves. They exemplify optimal engagement, moments where your skills and challenges were perfectly matched and resulted in memorable career/life success stories.

You may find it helpful to conceptualize your accomplishments as STAR stories; STAR is a widely used acronym for situation, task, action, and result. STAR stories will be useful as you work through the entire process of establishing and building your career, by gaining greater self-clarity, visioning, goal setting/planning, and implementing and adapting your approach. STAR stories may help you connect with your support system, begin to actively network, write your resume and coach your references, generate concrete leads, and respond to questions in job interviews. Therefore, it is well worth some time at this stage to organize your accomplishments into this format.

Tip You may need to use additional pages to list your accomplishments. Consider starting an "Accomplishment Diary," journal, social media account, or blog to create an ongoing record.

ACTIVITY 5.2 *STAR Story*

Draw from the same stories you used in the 5P exercise. Keep in mind that an effective STAR story does not have to be work related; it doesn't even have to be recent. Rather, the key to a STAR story is that it showcases how your transferable skills or competencies contributed to a significant accomplishment. To write a STAR story, follow these five simple steps:

1. Briefly describe the context of your story—the **situation**. Consider times when you won a trophy or an award. Reflect on thank-you letters, performance reviews, or positive feedback from others. Perhaps there was a time when you made a significant difference by doing something faster, better, or in a new way. Write down three situations as possibilities for your STAR stories. *Sandeep wrote, "Coordinating a volunteer fair."*

   _____

   _____

   _____

2. As you reflect on the situations you listed, what was your **task** at the time? What did you set out to accomplish? *Sandeep wrote, "Coordinate a volunteer fair for my internship, in partnership with another nonprofit organization in the community." For each of the situations listed in the previous section, use this space to briefly identify your goal or purpose.*

   _____

   _____

   _____

3. As the focus of a STAR story is your accomplishment, the next step is to identify the specific **actions** you took in the situations you described and the **attitudes** you exhibited. Using action verbs, describe what you did and how you did it. *Sandeep coordinated a volunteer fair by connecting with another community agency*

that had access to volunteers, planning an agenda, designing the space, writing social media content, creating posters, and tracking registrations through an invitation and registration app. He was enthusiastic, welcoming, and attentive to details.

_____

_____

_____

4. The **result** is the most important part of your STAR story as it represents your accomplishment. Focus on the outcome of your story and, where possible, quantify it. *Sandeep exceeded the association's attendance target by 20%; as a result of the volunteer fair, 30% more volunteers were recruited, filling several key previously unmet needs within the organization.* Use this space to record the results of your STAR stories.

_____

_____

_____

5. Some of these action statements may be useful for your resume. To convert a STAR story to a **resume bullet**, simply combine the specific action you took and the result. *Sandeep wrote, "Coordinated volunteer fair for a community agency, resulting in 30% increase in volunteers filling key unmet roles."* Record these bullets in a master resume—a document where you collect all information that may be helpful for a resume. You will draw relevant information from your master resume when you need to send a resume to a specific employer.

_____

_____

_____

Reflecting on the 5 Ps and writing out some of your STAR stories are great ways to identify your accomplishments. Another source of information is interviewing the people who know you best. The

Tip Use your STAR story resume bullets to get a master resume started; or, if you already have a master resume, add your STAR story bullets to it now.

advantage of asking others about your accomplishments is that they have a different perspective; that is, they can see you and your accomplishments against a backdrop of others doing similar activities. Many of us underestimate our strengths, believing "If I can do this, anybody could!" We tend to minimize or overlook significant accomplishments. Some people, on the other hand, have an exaggerated sense of their abilities, unaware that others have achieved similar or greater results.

Many organizations use a 360-degree feedback process to help their employees gain a more comprehensive perspective of their performance by soliciting feedback from others—such as supervisors, peers, direct reports, customers—who have observed their work. As you seek information about your own skills/competencies and accomplishments, ask people who know you well or who have supervised your work to provide you with specific feedback. Because different skills may shine in various life roles, be sure to ask for feedback from people who see you in different contexts; you might find it helpful to reach out to relatives, family friends, peers, coaches, instructors, mentors, supervisors, and colleagues.

Although you could gather this information through informal conversations, another strategy is to give your sources an opportunity to respond on paper or even anonymously, via an online survey. The questionnaire in the next activity is reproduced with permission from Ergon Communications.

ACTIVITY 5.3 *Significant Others Questionnaire*

Please complete the following questions. Your opinion is important to help [insert name] _____ make future career plans; therefore, your honesty is greatly appreciated.

1. What would you say this person is good at? What skills has this person demonstrated?

_____

_____

_____

2. What would you see as this person's major interest areas?

_____

_____

_____

3. How would you describe the personal characteristics of this person?

_____

_____

_____

4. What positive changes have you noticed over time in this person, especially in relation to work or looking for work?

_____

_____

_____

5. In what ways could this person continue to improve?

_____

_____

_____

6. What positive skills and attributes have you noticed about this person that might go unrecognized?

_____

---

7. If you were to suggest the ideal job or career prospect for this person, what would it be?

If you prefer to preserve anonymity, or if some of the individuals you would like to survey don't live or work nearby, it is very easy to set up free online surveys using sites such as Survey Monkey. Send a survey link by e-mail and use the body of the e-mail to update your contacts about your current status, for example, in school, about to graduate, trying to decide on a major, or looking for part-time work. This type of networking can produce helpful insights and specific job leads. As you introduce your survey, explain its purpose—for example, to help you clarify your career goals—and ask for honest feedback based on the respondents' observations. Your survey questions could ask about respondents' perceptions of your strengths, skills, or challenges as well as their suggestions for possible careers, areas of study, or relevant contacts. Aim to survey 5–10 people to generate enough data for themes to emerge. Request that your survey be completed by a specific date. For short surveys, allowing a few days is enough time; leaving the survey open for longer makes it tempting to set the e-mail aside, and it may get buried in a long list of "to-do" items.

After analyzing your survey results, thank your contacts and inform them about career decisions you have made. This keeps your network actively engaged in supporting your career development. You will likely find the same people helpful in the visioning, goal setting/planning, and implementing and adapting stages of this hope-action approach to career development. As an added benefit, their positive feedback and support will likely help to sustain your hope, an essential element at the heart of the process.

Of course, not all of the survey results will be positive; you've asked for honest feedback and Question 5 inquires specifically about areas for improvement. Therefore, it's important not to get defensive or take the feedback too personally. Although it can be hard to step back and take an objective look at critical feedback, you will likely find some kernel of truth in it. Learning to accept and value feedback is an important employability skill and will serve you well in future performance reviews.

To supplement the information you've gathered from others about what they see as your skills, review any previous lists of transferable skills that you completed. Live Career provides a comprehensive list of transferable skills at www.livecareer.com/career/advice/jobs/transferable-skills-set. O*NET also has a useful list and is directly linked to occupational codes and descriptions; you'll find it at online.onetcenter.org/skills/. There are also several frameworks identifying essential competencies to facilitate successful school-to-work transitions and lifelong career success. One example, from Canada, comprises six competencies: critical thinking and problem solving; innovation, creativity, and entrepreneurship; learning to learn/self-awareness and self-direction; collaboration; communication; and global citizenship and sustainability. They are described at www.cmec.ca/682/Global_Competencies.html.

ACTIVITY 5.4 *Data Mining Transferable Skills*

You've likely already realized that information about your transferable skills will come from many different sources, not just work experience. Similar to other research involving data from diverse sources, it is important to effectively organize, synthesize, and analyze your transferable skills data and then translate them into language useful to a potential employer. Data mining techniques can be helpful at this stage.

For this activity, you'll need internet access to the O*NET site: online.onetcenter.org/. If you don't have internet access, consider using print resources—such as job descriptions, advertisements, or performance reviews—to find examples of workplace language.

To begin, you'll need an organizational framework. At the simplest level, create a table. In the first column, list the transferable skills you've already identified. In the second column, rename your skills (if required) into language used by employers (to get familiar with this language, read job descriptions that interest you and read occupational descriptions at O*NET). In the third column, briefly describe evidence of the skill and where you developed or demonstrated it. An example follows for Sandeep; for this example, we're assuming that Sandeep is interested in a career in human resource management, which his research has indicated will have lots of job openings in the next several years and immediate needs, especially within recruiting, once the pandemic-related "stay home" order is lifted. We have used the O*NET descriptions for this occupation to translate his skills into relevant workplace language. After his example, use the table to fill in your own skills and evidence.

Sample: Sandeep's Transferable Skills/Competencies

TRANSFERABLE SKILL/COMPETENCY	WORKPLACE LANGUAGE	EVIDENCE
Active listening	Paying attention to what others are saying; asking appropriate questions	Successful volunteer fair developed based on hearing information about unmet needs and reaching out to another community organization that could provide volunteers
Complex problem solving	Identifying problems, reviewing relevant information, implementing solutions	Event coordinator for volunteer fair; set up successful volunteer fair that resulted in recruiting 30% more volunteers to fill critical unmet needs
Establishing and maintaining interpersonal relationships	Developing effective working relationships with others, connecting people to each other	Good letters of reference; maintained network of international students; connected two community agencies to recruit and place volunteers to fulfill important roles

Now it's your turn; complete the following table.

Your Transferable Skills/Competencies

TRANSFERABLE SKILL/COMPETENCY	WORKPLACE LANGUAGE	EVIDENCE

ACTIVITY 5.5 *Skills I Most Want to Use at Work*

As you reflect on your skills—using these checklists, your own reflections, your resume, and your 360-degree survey or significant others questionnaire as prompts—consider which skills you are most motivated to use at work (i.e., which skills are most likely to contribute to your job satisfaction and career success). Use the space provided to write down the 10–15 skills you most want to use at work. *Sandeep learned that he has many skills that will be valuable to future employers. Those skills that he is most motivated to use at work include organizing events or workshops, liaising, making connections, and influencing HR policies and procedures to make the workplace better in practical ways.*

_____

_____

_____

_____

_____

_____

_____

_____

_____

_____

_____

_____

_____

_____

Benchmarking Skills Against Others

Once you have identified the transferable skills you would like to incorporate into your career, benchmark those skills. Benchmarking is a method of comparing something to an exemplar or best practice—for example, finding a great example of a specific skill/competency and then comparing your current abilities to that benchmark. To begin, select people successful in the field or specific occupation that you hope to build your career in. To identify successful people, consider those you met at career fairs, guest speakers in your courses, instructors, family friends, or people you have seen on TV, followed on social media, or read about in magazines. Observe their use of the skills you identified; if possible, set up an informational interview to talk with them about those skills and how they acquired them. For example, like Sandeep, you may have identified skill and interest in making presentations. However, as you benchmark that skill, you may notice a considerable difference between an instructor teaching a class at the university, a speaker at an orientation session you attended at school, a presidential lecture, and a motivational speaker at a public event with thousands in the audience. Benchmarking will help you to identify the subtle differences between "making presentations" in each of those roles. How will your existing skills need to be polished or further developed to move you to the next stage in your career?

Some skills are considered foundational or essential. Many governments and employer groups have created lists of such skills and all tend to include basic literacy such as reading, writing, speaking, listening, and numeracy; learning and innovation; social/relational skills, including cultural competency; technical skills; critical thinking, problem-solving, and decision-making skills; and personal qualities such as self-management. As you reflect on your skills, do not overlook the basics. The P21 Partnership for 21st Century Learning[1] website, provides a detailed overview of skills students need today.

> **ACTIVITY 5.6** *Foundational or Essential Skills*
>
> Use the table to specify five skills/competencies that will be important no matter what kind of work you may do. Next, identify one strategy for further developing each skill. Use the last column in the table to outline how you can demonstrate each skill to a potential employer.

---

1   http://www.p21.org/our-work/p21-framework

Sample: Sandeep's Foundational or Essential Skills/Competencies

IMPORTANT SKILLS/ COMPETENCIES	STRATEGIES FOR DEVELOPING SKILLS	IDEAS FOR DEMONSTRATING SKILLS TO POTENTIAL EMPLOYERS
1. Working with others	Continue to find creative ways to connect with team while working virtually; join an association outside of school	Add a resume bullet to detail an accomplishment from working on a team
2. Bilingual	Continue to meet with HR team daily, using Zoom; initiate calls with local friends from school to strengthen English; speak to friends and family in India, on the phone or with Skype, to strengthen Punjabi	Ensure there are no grammatical errors on resume or cover letter; highlight ability to speak two languages on resume; practice responding to potential interview questions
3. Computer use	Take a course to become more familiar with some Microsoft products such as Excel and OneNote	Add a resume bullet to describe specific computer projects (e.g., tracking volunteer fair registrations on a customized Excel spreadsheet; using MS Word templates to create compelling posters)
4. Critical thinking	Get more involved with problem solving and decision making on HR projects during internship	Prepare to discuss specific examples of critical thinking in response to interview questions such as "Tell me about a time when you realized that the traditional way of doing something wasn't going to work"

IMPORTANT SKILLS/ COMPETENCIES	STRATEGIES FOR DEVELOPING SKILLS	IDEAS FOR DEMONSTRATING SKILLS TO POTENTIAL EMPLOYERS
5. Organizational skills	Create schedules for staying active and filling skills gaps, even when restricted to working from home during the pandemic; look ahead to final term for assignment due dates; use calendar, prioritizing flags and task reminders in Outlook	Ensure portfolio is organized effectively and resume and cover letter are attractively formatted and clearly written; be on time for interview

Now it's your turn; complete the following table.

Your Foundational or Essential Skills/Competencies

IMPORTANT SKILLS	STRATEGIES FOR DEVELOPING SKILLS	IDEAS FOR DEMONSTRATING SKILLS TO POTENTIAL EMPLOYERS
1.		
2.		
3.		
4.		
5.		

Conducting a Gap Analysis

Through the activities in this chapter, you have likely identified a rich collection of transferable skills and competencies that will be relevant to your future employers. However, through benchmarking and reading occupational descriptions in resources such as O*NET, you may also have identified some gaps. Look for opportunities to strategically fill those through taking courses or attending webinars, volunteer activities, or paid employment. For example, if you've identified a need to demonstrate critical thinking skills, just as Sandeep did, offer to serve on an advisory group within your community. If your written communication needs practice, offer to contribute to a newsletter and invite critical feedback from peers and reviewers. If you are uncomfortable speaking to groups, offer to take the lead in presenting your next group project or prepare a short presentation for coworkers on a relevant topic.

Tip To fill skill gaps, look for opportunities to develop those skills, even though it may seem counterintuitive to volunteer for something you're not yet very good at.

ACTIVITY 5.7 *Gap Analysis and Skill Development Strategies*

Use the space provided to list five skill gaps you've identified and two or three strategies to build skills in each of those areas.

SKILL GAP	TWO TO THREE STRATEGIES

Implementing Strategies to Develop the Skills You Need

Through your surveys, invited feedback, and benchmarking, you may have received some critical feedback or have identified skill deficits or weaknesses that aren't easily or quickly resolved. In preparation for interviews or coaching conversations with supervisors, consider how you might be able to reframe some of those criticisms into compliments. For example, if you are known for doing things at the last minute, you have likely developed strong competencies that support working under very tight deadlines or working under pressure. If you're shy, you likely work very well with minimal supervision and you're not easily distracted. In the space provided, list three criticisms and a reasonable reframe for each. In Sandeep's case, he already knows he will be criticized for his limited work experience and, realistically, he can't just invent experience for his resume. However, he can come to the interview prepared to provide evidence of the skills he developed through his volunteer and internship experiences.

ACTIVITY 5.8 *Reframing Criticisms*

Use the space provided to list three criticisms that may come up in an interview. For each of those criticisms, write a plausible reframe— that is, turn the criticism into a compliment or provide compelling evidence of how you can work effectively despite that gap.

_____

_____

_____

_____

_____

_____

_____

Prioritizing Skills/Competencies to Showcase

Throughout the activities and reflections in this chapter, it's quite likely that you've surfaced some skills and competencies that you'd prefer not to use at work (or might be willing to use but not as a primary part of your role). As your career grows and develops, you may want to set some of your skills aside, temporarily or permanently, as you focus on integrating new skills into your day-to-day work.

Use the space provided to list any skills that you'd prefer not to become the primary focus of your next position. Keep this list handy when writing or editing your social media profiles, resume, cover letters, or portfolios. Some social media apps (e.g., LinkedIn) provide opportunities for others to endorse you for specific skills. Be strategic about the skills that you don't want to highlight—and also about prioritizing those that you do want to form a significant part of your future roles and responsibilities at work.

_____

_____

_____

_____

_____

Summary

Sandeep, introduced in the case example in this chapter, is relieved to know he can showcase his rich school and life experiences to illustrate skills that employers are looking for. He has learned to speak about his skills in language that employers use and has organized his resume and career portfolio to ensure that his skills catch employers' attention long before they notice that he doesn't have much paid work experience. He has also identified several creative ways to fill his time during the unexpected "stay home" lockdown due to the COVID-19 pandemic. He has found that having a focus and using this time to put things in place for when the economy resumes has helped him feel better and given him concrete reasons to stay connected to family and friends, reducing his isolation and calming the anxiety he was feeling.

Throughout the activities and reflections in this chapter, you have systematically gathered information about your skills and competencies; this is an important step in enhancing your self-clarity. Mapping accomplishments and transferable skills and getting positive feedback from significant others can bolster your belief (your hope) that you'll qualify for the work you apply for. Realistically identifying and addressing skill gaps or deficits at this point in your career planning process provides sufficient time to strategically fill those gaps. This will be much more challenging if you wait until you actively look for work. You can further support your quest for self-clarity by examining your personal style, values, and sources of support.

Questions for Reflection and Discussion

1. Sandeep was able to identify several transferable skills despite his lack of formal work experience (see sample in Activity 5.4). Reflect on some of your own nonwork experiences and identify transferable skills from those experiences.

2. Identify a specific skill you would like to develop. Identify three different ways to develop that skill and the tangible evidence that will confirm you have acquired it. If you find yourself stuck for creative ideas, consult with a friend, colleague, mentor, coach, or member of your family to generate some possibilities for skill development.

3. Visit the O*NET website (www.onetonline.org/find//). Select one job family that interests you and then click on one specific occupation. Read the description. Reflect on your experience so far and on how you could provide evidence of the skills required. Consider how you might make a case for your qualifications for the job on your resume and in an interview.

Reference

Magnusson, K. (2001). *Highlight: Career conversations and the 5Ps*. http://life-role. com/documents/Summary%20-%205Ps.pdf

Additional Resources

Kim, L. (2015). *3 ways to discover your hidden natural talent*. Inc. https://www.inc. com/leonard-kim/how-to-discover-the-hidden-talents-that-will-make-you-a-business-star.html

> This article introduces three key insights to uncover natural talents from the founder of StrengthsLauncher, Doug Wilks. These simple self-reflective

exercises will help illuminate joyful activities from grade school that can be integrated into your career path ahead.

Mind Tools. (n.d.). *Test your skill!* MindTools. https://www.mindtools.com/pages/article/get-started.htm

> This 5-minute quiz can identify several different skills areas of importance to you (i.e., leadership and management, problem solving and decision making, communication, time management, and personal mastery). Extend your reflection by visiting the suggested resources for each skill set.

Morin, A. (2017, January 29). *7 ways to talk about your accomplishments without sounding like a braggart.* Forbes. https://www.forbes.com/sites/amymorin/2017/01/29/7-ways-to-talk-about-your-accomplishments-without-sounding-like-a-braggart/#183b10d36fcc

> When reflecting on your skills, there is a careful balance to strike between bragging and being too modest. This article provides seven helpful ways to communicate your accomplishments in an authentic, humble way.

Yate, M. (2018, February 9). *The 7 transferable skills to help you change careers.* Forbes. https://www.forbes.com/sites/nextavenue/2018/02/09/the-7-transferable-skills-to-help-you-change-careers/#332e9a984c04

> This article defines transferable skills as those which are foundational to your career success and common to every job and workplace. They include technical, communication, critical thinking, multitasking, teamwork, creativity, and leadership.

6 PERSONALITY STYLE

This chapter focuses on personality as an important component of career choice. After reading and completing activities in this chapter, you will be able to do the following:

- Assess your personal style by combining self-assessment and the perspectives of others

- Understand the strengths and limitations of your personal style

- Understand how each aspect of personal style can be applied effectively, overused, or underused

CASE EXAMPLE

Melinda and Flo are good friends and were both working with the airlines. With the health crisis, they became unemployed and are now in a position where they are looking for alternate types of work. As part of an unemployment initiative, they have enrolled in a career development seminar and are considering other career alternatives.

The two women have very different backgrounds. Melinda's parents were missionaries and she also hopes someday to become a missionary. She is a nurturing person and tries to help out wherever she can. Flo was born in Malaysia and has been living in the United States for fifteen years. Her father works at a university as an instructor. Her mother died of cancer when she was 12 years old and she has been helping to care for three younger siblings. She is bright and is interested in retraining possibilities.

Melinda is gregarious and loves meeting new people, particularly those from other cultures. She speaks up in groups and isn't afraid to disagree with people in authority. Flo, on the other hand is more reserved and keeps to herself. She is conscientious and everything she does is done well.

As part of the career development course, Melinda and Flo complete a personal style survey. The results of the survey highlight their different personality profiles, and this and other information help Melinda decide to continue pursuing a career in the travel or hospitality industry while Flo makes plans to return to higher education.

This chapter focuses on the personality dimensions and starts with a short assessment process. There are many ways to assess personality, and most of them involve choosing from a list of characteristics and then transforming this information into some form of personality profile. While this can be a useful activity, it focuses only on the way in which you look at yourself. It can be even more helpful to incorporate the opinions of others along with your own self-assessment. With this in mind, go through the five-step assessment process in this chapter. (Note: This assessment process is based on the instrument Individual Style Survey by Dr. Norman Amundson, and it was originally published by Psychometrics Canada. More information on the availability of the instrument is included at the end of the chapter.) Start by doing a self-assessment, and then consult with other people who know you in different settings (e.g., in your class, at home, in your leisure time, and so on). Taken together, these ratings will provide some interesting and helpful information.

Personal Style Assessment

ACTIVITY 6.1 *Personal Style Assessment*

Step one: Assessing yourself

In this self-assessment eight personal style adjectives are listed along with a brief definition. Make sure that you take the time to consider both the word and the definition. You will note that all the definitions are written in a positive slant, an indication that each of these personality characteristics can be useful in certain situations. What you want to note is which descriptors fit you most of the time. Rank order the terms, starting with the two that are most like you, continuing through the list to the two descriptors least like you. Listed are the personal descriptors.

Personal descriptors

Spontaneous: I am instinctive and act on my impulses.

Analytical: I am careful and critical and strive for accuracy.

Outgoing: I am energetic and expressive and enjoy talking to people.

Reserved: I am sensitive and quiet and generally keep my thoughts and feeling to myself.

Assertive: I am open and forthright in expressing my ideas and feelings.

Patient: I am tolerant, calm, and willing to let situations run their natural course.

Forceful: I have clear ideas and take action to get things done.

Empathic: I am sympathetic and understanding and respond easily to the feelings of others.

Here is how Melinda rank ordered these descriptors:

Top two descriptors:

Spontaneous, Outgoing (assigned a score of 4)

She then chose the following, in order:

Empathic, Assertive (assigned a score of 3)

Forceful, Analytical (assigned a score of 2)

Patient, Reserved (assigned a score of 1)

Now it is your turn to do your own self-assessment.

SELF-APPRAISAL FORM

Read the following descriptors and then choose the two most like you, continuing through the list to the two descriptors least like you.

Personal descriptors

Spontaneous: I am instinctive and act on my impulses.

Analytical: I am careful and critical and strive for accuracy.

Outgoing: I am energetic and expressive and enjoy talking to people.

Reserved: I am sensitive and quiet and generally keep my thoughts and feeling to myself.

Assertive: I am open and forthright in expressing my ideas and feelings.

Patient: I am tolerant, calm, and willing to let situations run their natural course.

Forceful: I have clear ideas and take action to get things done.

Empathic: I am sympathetic and understanding and respond easily to the feelings of others.

From the eight descriptors, write the two which are most like you:

_____ (4) _____

From the six descriptors left, write the two that are next most like you:

_____ (3) _____

From the four descriptors left, write the two that are more like you:

_____ (2) _____

Write the remaining two descriptors:

_____ (1) _____

Step two: Getting assessments from others

Now that you have completed your self-assessment it is time to think about whom you might ask to provide an assessment of your personality. Consider asking family members, friends, classmates, coworkers, employers, teachers, and so on. Try to choose people who know you in different settings. Generally we would recommend giving it to at least three other people, but you might want to vary this according to your own situation. Don't show others how you have assessed yourself. What you want to know is how they assess you and how this compares to your own ratings. Make some copies of the form and give it to the people you have selected.

Margin Note. Sometimes it is interesting to involve some people who know you very well and others who might know you in a more limited context.

OTHER PERSON APPRAISAL FORM

The person who has given you this form is doing an individual style survey. When assessing one's style it is important to have a number of viewpoints. You have been asked for your input because it is felt that your views would be helpful. Your cooperation in providing this information is appreciated.

Read carefully the following descriptors and then choose the two most like the person who has given you this form, continuing through the list to the two descriptors least like the person.

Personal descriptors

Spontaneous: He or she is instinctive and acts on impulses.

Analytical: He or she is careful and critical and strives for accuracy.

Outgoing: He or she is energetic and expressive and enjoys talking to people.

Reserved: He or she is sensitive and quiet and generally keeps thoughts and feeling to his- or herself.

Assertive: He or she is open and forthright in expressing ideas and feelings.

Patient: He or she is tolerant, calm, and willing to let situations run their natural course.

Forceful: He or she has clear ideas and takes action to get things done.

Empathic: He or she is sympathetic and understanding and responds easily to the feelings of others.

From the eight descriptors, write the two which best describe him or her:

_____ (4) _____

From the remaining six descriptors, write the two that next describe him or her:

_____ (3) _____

From the remaining four descriptors, write the two that somewhat describe him or her:

_____ (2) _____

Write the remaining two descriptors:

_____ (1) _____

Note: When you have completed this form please return it to the person who asked you to fill it out.

Step three: Scoring

Listed is an explanation of how to score the information you have collected. There are three calculations that need to be made:

1. First calculation

Start by organizing the scores for each descriptor by adding together personal scores and scores from other people. Continuing with Melinda's example, she gave her other person forms to Flo, her father, and an uncle who was close to her. They ranked her as follows:

Flo: (4) Spontaneous, Outgoing; (3) Assertive, Empathic; (2) Analytical, Forceful; (1) Reserved, Patient

Father: (4) Spontaneous, Analytical; (3) Outgoing, Assertive; (2) Forceful, Empathic; (1) Reserved, Patient

Uncle: (4) Outgoing, Assertive; (3) Spontaneous, Forceful; (2) Analytical, Empathic; (1) Reserved, Patient

Spontaneous: Self – 4	Others – 4, 4, and 3	Total: 15
Analytical: Self – 2	Others – 2, 4, and 2	Total: 10
Outgoing: Self – 4	Others – 4, 3, and 4	Total: 15
Reserved: Self – 1	Others – 1, 1, and 1	Total: 4
Assertive: Self – 3	Others – 3, 3, and 4	Total: 13
Patient: Self – 1	Others – 1, 1, and 1	Total: 4
Forceful: Self – 2	Others – 2, 2, and 3	Total: 9
Empathic: Self – 3	Others – 3, 2, and 2	Total: 10

Now it is your turn; calculate your scores for each of the descriptors:

Spontaneous:

Analytical:

Outgoing:

Reserved:

Assertive:

Patient:

Forceful:

Empathic:

2. Second calculation:

These eight descriptors can be further organized into four major themes using the following formula:

Influencing = Spontaneous + Outgoing

Harmonious = Empathic + Patient

Action Oriented = Assertive + Forceful

Prudent = Reserved + Analytical

Using this framework for Melinda, she would have the following scores:

Influencing: 15 + 15 = 30

Harmonious: 4 + 10 = 14

Action oriented: 13 + 9 = 22

Prudent: 4 + 10 = 14

Now do the calculations for your scores on these four themes:

Influencing:

Harmonious:

Action oriented:

Prudent:

3. Third calculation:

One final calculation can be done by organizing the scores according to the following formula:

People = Influencing + Harmonious

Task = Prudent + Action Oriented

Interactive = Influencing + Action Oriented

Introspective = Harmonious + Prudent

Using Melinda as the example, her scores on these themes would be the following:

People: 30 + 14 = 44

Task: 14 + 22 = 36

Interactive: 30 + 22 = 52

Introspective: 14 + 14 = 28

Now it is your turn to do this final calculation.

    People:

    Task:

    Interactive:

    Introspective:

Step four: Analysis

Now that you have completed the assessment portion, the big question is "So what does this all mean?" As a starting point it is helpful to look at the individual scores and identify any situation where there is at least a two-point differential. For example, with Melinda she rated herself as a two on analytical, Flo gave her a 3, her father a 4, and her uncle a 2. It might be interesting for Melinda to discuss with her father why he rated her so high on analytical. It is not a matter of being right or wrong; it is just a different perspective, and it is important to understand more fully the rationale for the difference. Because this is a very "rough" instrument there is little point in dwelling on one-point differences; you really need to have at least a two-point differential to discuss differences in perspective.

Strengths and limitations of style profiles

It is important that you understand your style profile with its overall strengths and limitations. As with most things, it is important to access strengths and work on areas that are less developed. Think about how these factors apply to your personal life and to your educational and work situations. High scores in a certain area indicate a sense of comfort and ease with a particular range of behavior. Conversely, low scores may indicate a lack of usage of some style areas. If your scores are quite close together it might mean that you move back and forth between the two personality domains.

Adapted from: Norman Amundson, "Individual Styles Survey." Copyright © 1999 by Norman Amundson. Reprinted with permission.

ACTIVITY 6.2 *Strengths and Limitations of Personality Styles*

1. What does it mean to be high in Harmonious, Influencing, Action oriented or Prudent? Divide into groups based on your highest scores (make four groups if possible). Consider how your strength in a particular area helps you and also how it might hinder you (a blind spot) in some situations. Also, think of some potentially attractive careers that fit with your theme.

2. Form new groups based on the lowest scores. What insights can be derived by considering this perspective?

It is helpful to consider the relative strengths and weaknesses of the various theme areas. Each style has a certain range (context) in which it is effective and also some situations in which it is ineffective. Perhaps the metaphor of driving a car with a standard gear shift might be helpful in clarifying this process. A person needs to shift gears in response to different situations. Problems occur when one stays in the same gear for too long, or when one shifts to a gear that is not appropriate for the situation. Thus, personality is not a fixed entity but something that moves about in relation to different situations. What is important is that people are able to incorporate effective "style shifting." When we are engaged in career flow we are smoothly and appropriately using the various style domains.

By really understanding this information you will be better able to relate with others. For example, suppose you wanted to present and get support for a new idea. When approaching someone with a strong prudent style, you would need to present a detailed and well-organized plan. For someone

Tip In reviewing your personality profile, focus on how easy it is for you to slip from one style to another depending on the needs of the situation. Effective communication depends on style flexibility

with a harmonious style, you may need to stress that your idea falls within accepted guidelines and would not be overly disruptive. A person with a strong influencing style would be most interested in the overall plan and might be particularly attracted to the marketing possibilities. From an action oriented style perspective, a high value would be placed on the "bottom line" and measurable benefits.

The last part of this chapter is focused on helping you to better understand how the various styles can be effectively used as well as overused and underused. In reviewing this material think about your profile and focus on both your strengths and potential weaknesses.

Effective Use, Overuse, and Underuse of Personal Style

Action Oriented

Effective Use: Action Oriented

When you use your action-oriented style appropriately, it can lead to assertive and decisive actions. You are able to speak clearly and take bold steps, which requires courage and foresight. You have the strength of character to make an unpopular decision and the resolve to carry it through. You rely on your own powers of analysis to sort through the confusion that may surround you. You are a builder and won't quit until the job is completed.

Overuse: Action Oriented

If you are strong in being action oriented you may tend to use this style in excess and find that you are "coming on too strong." Rather than a healthy assertiveness, your behavior may take on aggressive tones. You may resort to bullying people when you don't get your way. You may also be stubborn and unreasonably resist any change in your approach. When in this mode you are very susceptible to your power needs and may push ahead with little regard to the feelings of others. You become like a "bulldozer" and while things are accomplished you may end up creating more problems for yourself.

Underuse: Action Oriented

In situations where you do not employ an action-oriented style when it would be appropriate you may find yourself unfulfilled, doing the work of others, and unable to follow your own wishes. You may secretly feel resentful, but your good manners prevent you from saying anything. You may also find yourself rationalizing why things are turning out the way they are. Your failure to act leaves you helpless and in the service of others. As a result, you may have difficulty winning respect and find that you are being taken for granted.

Influencing

Effective Use: Influencing

When your influencing style is used appropriately, it can be a powerful means of moving people to action through persuasion rather than coercion. You are energetic and inspiring and confidently express your opinions. You also have a twinkle in your eye and a good sense of humor. This allows you to deal with difficult situations and people with relative ease. You have innovative ideas and can see new ways of solving problems. People are attracted to you and you have a wide circle of friends.

Overuse: Influencing

If you rely too heavily on this style, you may find yourself relying on your verbal skills to get you through any situation. Rather than doing the necessary background preparation, you may push ahead with poorly conceived and disorganized plans. As a result, you leave yourself open to charges of superficiality and inconsistency. When in this mode you are very susceptible to your attention and recognition needs and may do or say things to keep the "spotlight" on yourself. As a result, you may overlook the needs of others and create resentments. There is also the temptation to use your persuasive skills to manipulate others. While there may be some short-term gains, the end result is usually negative.

Underuse: Influencing

You are unable to express your ideas with clarity and confidence. You feel embarrassed speaking in front of others and are uncomfortable with large groups. You tend to notice the missing details and logical inconsistencies in arguments, but by the time you have carefully formulated your ideas the discussion may have shifted to another topic. It is often easier to be silent rather than make a public statement. Even when you do speak your mind, you may find that people don't seem to really appreciate your ideas. You feel frustrated and powerless in social situations.

Effective Use: Harmonious

When you are appropriately using this style you listen empathically to the concerns of others and deal with problems in a fair and compassionate manner. In your relationships with others you are positive and encouraging. In stressful situations you are calm and rational and make decisions that are in the best interest of everyone concerned. You work to create a harmonious environment and people can depend on your good will.

Overuse: Harmonious

If you are strong in this style, you may find that you are too patient and concerned about the welfare of others. You may have difficulty making "tough" decisions, even if it is for the benefit of the other person. You may also have difficulty being objective and find yourself being too lenient with evaluations. You will tend to take the problems of others home with you and this will be hard on you (burnout) and your friends and family. In this mode you are very susceptible to your need to be needed (nurturance). By being too sympathetic and patient you become ineffective in your helping.

Underuse: Harmonious

In situations where you do not use this style when it would be appropriate you will find yourself impatient and unconcerned about the needs of others. You may be anxious to get moving ahead and do not feel that you have the time or interest to be concerned with how people are feeling. You are only concerned with results and can't understand why others don't approach tasks with the same straightforward approach. You are anxious to achieve results and place your emphasis on action rather than exploration and defining the problem. By adopting this approach you may achieve some quick results but create additional problems for yourself in the process.

Effective Use: Prudent

When you are appropriately using this mode you are thoughtful and careful about quality. You are able to take an idea and work out a detailed action plan. You don't get swept away with change for the sake of change. You are disciplined in your approach and stick to methods that have proven them-selves to be effective over a period of time. You let your actions speak for themselves and don't waste your time boasting about your accomplishments.

Overuse: Prudent

If you overextend your use of this style you will find that your focus on details will result in a loss of perspective on the bigger picture. There is a saying that you may "see the trees but miss the forest." Your need for precision may hamper your ability to act quickly and decisively. Your analysis may take too long and opportunities will pass you by. In addition to overanalyzing situations, you may find that you are misunderstood because you are too quiet. Your silence may be interpreted as disinterest or a lack of initiative.

Underuse: Prudent

In situations where you are not cautious when it would be appropriate you may find yourself "badly burned." In your hurry to move ahead you may miss essential details and suffer the consequences later. You may find yourself speaking without sufficient thought and analysis. While everyone likes a quick answer or solution, your "off-the-cuff" comments may lack consistency and depth. If this persists, your reputation will be tarnished and you may find yourself without support, even when your ideas are solid.

People/Task

Effective Use of People and Task

The effective use of this style results in a comfortable mix between being on task and being sensitive to personal needs and to the needs of others. You are able to manage your time in such a way that you meet your objectives but also have time and energy for relationships with the people around you. You have a flexible schedule and are able to adjust your time to handle the unexpected. You basically have control over how you are spending your time and people respect you for not only what you accomplish, but also how you go about doing it.

Overuse of People/Underuse of Task

Your enjoyment of relationships may be strained by your inability to meet obligations and goals. You may have difficulties staying on track and find yourself easily distracted by people and new situations. In this particular mode you are susceptible to procrastination and insufficient attention to detail. Your focus on people may lead to underachievement, superficiality, and poor-quality work. You may find yourself "run off your feet" with commitments to others and with insufficient time and energy to meet your own personal goals.

Underuse People/Overuse Task

You become so focused on meeting objectives and deadlines that you bypass your working colleagues and other important people in your life. While you may be making some gains in terms of production, you may be taking some losses in terms of personal relationships. People may avoid you because of your inflexibility, bluntness and/or critical feedback. When people approach you, they may be on their guard and be wary of sharing any personal concerns or weaknesses.

Introspective/Interactive

Effective Use of Both Introspective and Interactive

An effective blend of introspection and interaction allows you to obtain recognition for the quality work that you produce. Your talents and personality are visible to all, but this is accomplished within a context of modesty and humility. You are able to openly give and receive praise and are able to benefit from constructive feedback. People appreciate what you have to say because it is clear and well thought out.

Overuse Introspective/Underuse Interactive

Your unwillingness to openly express yourself may influence the perceptions of others. Your shyness and passivity may be interpreted as a lack of vision or ability. You may find yourself being taken for granted with few opportunities coming your way. People may take advantage of your generosity and quietness and leave you with much of the work, but few of the rewards. You have strong feelings about how you are being treated, but it is easier to withdraw than to directly confront the situation.

Underuse Introspective/Overuse Interactive

You are very visible in terms of your opinions and actions. Unfortunately, you have not always thought through the basis for your arguments and thus can be accused of being superficial and unprepared. You have a tendency to speak too quickly and far too forcefully. People may feel that you are pushy and only interested in being the center of attention. As a result, you may face direct or indirect resistance as you attempt to put your position forward.

Summary

This chapter focused on a personality assessment method that incorporates both self-assessment and the perspectives of others. This integrated approach provides an opportunity for discussion of differences between self-perceptions and how people are viewed in different contexts.

All of the personality components are viewed as being helpful in some situations and not so helpful in others. Effective communication requires the ability to shift styles depending on the requirements of the situation. Each style component has an effective use, an overuse, and an underuse. When career flow is operative there is a smooth movement between the various personality domains. The image of shifting gears in a car is good illustration of how personality shifts need to made in response to the demands of different situations.

Questions for Reflection and Discussion

1. Even though Melinda and Flo are in the same career field, they have very different personalities. How might these differences influence the career decisions they make?

2. Does a career in the travel industry allow people with very different personalities (such as Melinda and Flo) to find satisfaction in the field? If so, how can this be applied to other career options?

3. Suppose that two people completed the personality assessment exercise and had identical scores in all areas. Would this necessarily mean that they would respond the same in all instances? Apply the concept of style shifting in considering this question.

4. How does the notion of personal style fit with working in a group context? Can you think of situations where your style profile might be an asset and a situation where it might create a problem?

UNDERSTANDING VALUES THROUGH WORKPLACE ATTRACTION

7

OBJECTIVES

. . . .

This chapter focuses on the 10-factor workplace attraction model. After reading and completing activities in this chapter, you will be able to do the following:

- Assess the relative importance of various workplace attractors

- Identify how workplace attractors change over time

CASE EXAMPLE

. . . .

Jill is a young woman with a degree in sociology but who isn't that concerned about what kind of work she might do. She has been working in the travel industry, but with the current economic upheaval she finds herself unemployed and looking for other options. Through some family connections, she has a couple of opportunities in the pharmaceutical industry.

One of the options is a position in a pharmaceutical company where she would be working with a small team in a sales capacity, traveling to several nearby cities and presenting new products to a list of existing customers. One of the advantages of this position is that she could continue living at home while she gets herself established. She also has a friend who would be starting with her in a similar position.

The other job is also with a pharmaceutical firm, and though it pays higher and has some possibility for advancement, it is not close to home and thus she would need to relocate to a new area. With this position she would have more responsibility and would have her own office in a large warehouse. She would be responsible for keeping a record of supplies and ensuring that suffi-cient product is always on hand for direct sales and for online orders.

The decision that Jill faces is unique to her situation, but there are many occasions when people are faced with similar dilemmas about which pathway to follow. These situations present many complexities, and it is important for people to also think about their values and how these values will be reflected in the decision-making process.

Factors Associated With the Workplace Attractor Model

One way of considering values in a more holistic and comprehensive fashion is to use a workplace attractor model (Amundson, 2018). This approach uses a wide variety of values and is based on the metaphor of "magnetic attraction" as a reflection of the career choice process. People generally find themselves more attracted to certain career options. There is also attraction from the organization perspective where the organization is attracted to certain kinds of candidates. In a best-case scenario there is mutual attraction between the person and the organization.

The starting point for this model is identifying a series of attractors that might work for both individuals and organizations. In considering a number of different models (Herzberg et al., 1959; Ehrhart & Ziegert, 2005; Mitchell et al., 2001; Poehnell & Amundson, 2001; Schein, 1992; Schwartz et al. 2012; Super & Sverko, 1995) at least 10 different attractors play a major role with respect to workplace attraction (Amundson, 2007, 2018). These attractors are of differing significance for people, and they also can change over time. A brief description of the attractors follows.

Security

Security is a term that includes a broad range of tangible rewards for work-place services. These rewards could include items such as wages, benefits, and travel options. Other forms of security might focus on position security and/or emotional and physical safety.

Location

This refers to the place where the workplace is situated and also to the work environment aesthetics. There may be a convenience issue here as well as a desire to work in interesting and healthy work sites.

Relationships

This involves the interpersonal connections with coworkers, managers/supervisors, and clients or customers. There is a desire for relationships that are enjoyable, supportive, and fulfilling.

Recognition

This element refers to the ways in which people receive acknowledgement, status, and praise from others. Some examples of direct recognition include verbal praise, raises, certificates, and other "perks." There also are indirect ways of achieving recognition, for example working in a company with a good reputation.

Contribution

A sense of contribution comes from work that is meaningful and ethical and has a sense of purpose. There is a desire to be involved in activities that make a difference in the world/society.

Work Fit

Work fit focuses on the extent to which work is consistent with a person's existing skill set, their interests, personality, and values. A good match between the individual and the workplace usually ensures greater work satisfaction.

Flexibility

In a flexible workplace there is the opportunity to accommodate a variety of working arrangements (e.g., working at home, having variable schedules, taking advantage of customized benefit packages, having the opportunity for vacations and leaves). This flexibility is often directed toward greater work-life balance.

Learning

Learning is associated with involvement in a workplace that is challenging and that encourages lifelong skill development. Workplaces with an ongoing learning agenda support self-development and personal growth.

Responsibility

With responsibility comes autonomy and authority in handling work tasks. Greater responsibility is often associated with the opportunity to influence others through the application of leadership skills.

Innovation

With innovation comes the chance to have variety, to be original, and to build something new. Creative problem solving is often required, and there is the encouragement of the pioneering spirit.

FIGURE 7.1 *Workplace attractors.*

Assessing the Relative Importance of Workplace Attractors

ACTIVITY 7.1 *The Importance of Workplace Attractors*

How do the workplace attractors that have been presented fit with your feelings about working life and what you consider important? As a starting point, look over each of the attractors and in the space provided indicate how you would value each factor as you think about what is important to you in the workplace. For example, security may be important because everyone needs to have some assurance that they can meet their physical needs. At the same time, perhaps you have some family support that might make this less of an issue.

a. Security

_____

_____

_____

_____

b. Location

_____

_____

_____

_____

c. Relationships

_____

_____

_____

_____

d. Recognition

_____

_____

_____

_____

e. Contribution

_____

_____

_____

_____

f. Work fit

g. Flexibility

h. Learning

i. Responsibility

j. Innovation

k. Other (place here any additional points that you would like to add)

Tip As you consider various work options you may want to have conversations (information interviews) with people who are already working in these areas. This is often the only way to acquire a broad base of knowledge about working in a specific field.

ACTIVITY 7.2 *Rank Ordering Workplace Attractors*

Now that you have identified what the workplace attractors mean for you, take a moment to see if you can rank order what is important. One way to do this is to start by thinking about what you would be willing to give up if you really had to.

Which one can you take away? _____.

Once you have dropped one of the attractors try another one,

_____

and then a third _____

What are some of the feelings that you experience when you set certain factors aside?

_____

ACTIVITY 7.3 *Using a Pyramid to Assess Relative Importance*

Another way of assessing attractors is to create a pyramid for yourself. On the bottom level you can place the four attractors that are least important to you. Moving up the next level, you now place three attractors. And then there are the next two attractors, and finally the one that is most significant for you. Include your pyramid in the space provided.

_____

_____   _____

_____   _____   _____

_____   _____   _____   _____

There are no right or wrong answer to the pyramid that you have created. We are all unique and will have our own configuration.

The Changing Nature of Workplace Attractors

The workplace attractors that you have listed help to describe some of the important points that you need to consider when making your career choices. At the same time, this constellation of attractors should not be viewed as a static entity. Each person creates his or her own constellation of workplace influences at any given time (Hirschi, 2010; Locmele-Lunova & Cirjevskis, 2017; Wohrmann et al., 2016). This constellation shifts in response to life circumstances, cultural influences, and personal development. For example, health issues may play a key role in determining location and what level of security a person is willing to accept. Having children or other caretaking responsibilities might create a greater need for flexibility. Experiences in part-time or full-time work can influence how various attractors are valued. There also are indirect influences through viewing the experiences of others. With the downturn in the economy some people close to you may have experienced some stress in their work life. These experiences can play a part in shaping values and the relative importance of various workplace attractors.

ACTIVITY 7.4 *Changing Attractors*

List the ways in which various life experiences have changed the importance of some of the attractors for you. Give at least three examples:

1.

_____

_____

_____

2.

_____

_____

_____

3.

_____

_____

_____

Tip As attractors are shifting it can be important to communicate these changes to others. Changing jobs is one option, but there may also be other ways of meeting needs through a different work arrangement in the same firm.

Jill, the case example in this chapter, decided to take the pharmaceutical sales position and at first was happy with her decision but now is having second thoughts. The friend who started with her decided to get married and soon afterward moved to another city with her husband.

Jill also thought that the sales job would be mainly focusing on existing customers. The reality is that she is expected to do quite a bit of cold calling and she doesn't enjoy that part of the work. At the orientation she was with all the sales associates and that was enjoyable. However, now that she is actually doing the job she is mostly working on her own and this isn't really what she wanted. She is very sure that this is not a good long-term option for her. Staying at home has also presented some challenges. Jill is getting some real pressure from her parents to stay in the current position. Their thinking is that if she starts hopping from position to position it will reflect poorly on her reputation as a stable employee. They also have played a key role in creating these opportunities and don't want to create bad relationships with the people connected to the company where she is currently working.

The other pharmaceutical position that she was considering is still open and she wonders if maybe now is the time to make a change. If she acts quickly, she could give her notice and switch to the new position. She realizes that she needs a change and thinks that it might also be time to get her own place.

As you consider the various factors at play in this case scenario it is easy to see that there are some real differences between how her parents are viewing the situation and how Jill views her circumstances. One might also wonder how the employer(s) might view the situation. What becomes clear is that in any given scenario there can be very different perspectives, and these viewpoints might lead to misunderstandings and communication challenges.

Summary

How can you practically apply these exercises with workplace attractors to your values and to the career choices that you will be making? Most of the attractors have some appeal, and a key question might be how you will be able to acquire this information prior to making your choices. Usually the

location and security dimensions are easily determined, but it is more difficult to determine the other information. This is where research, information
interviewing, and asking questions in the interview come into play.

The following chapters will describe some strategies for acquiring this
additional information. You might also want to reflect on this process with
respect to your own career search.

Questions for Reflection and Discussion

1. Apply the workplace attractor model to the case illustration. What
   attractors seem to be highlighted in Jill's situation?

2. What advice would you give Jill as she prepares to move forward?

3. Think about the communication patterns between employers and
   workers. How might different attractor patterns lead to some mis-
   communication? Have you ever been in a situation where a different
   attractor pattern has led to some communication challenges?

References

Amundson, N. E. (2007). Workplace attractors. *Journal of Employment Counseling*,
   44(4), 154–162. https://doi.org/10.1002/j.2161-1920.2007.tb00034.x

Amundson, N. E. (2018). *Active engagement: The being and doing of career counselling*
   (Anniversary ed). Ergon Communications.

Ehrhart, K. H., & Ziegert, J. C. (2005). Why are individuals attracted to organizations?
   Journal of Management, *31*(6), 901–919. https://doi.org/10.1177/0149206305279759

Herzberg, F., Mausner, B., & Snyderman, B. B. (1959). *The motivation to work*. Wiley.

Hirschi, A. (2010). Positive adolescent career development: The role of intrinsic and
   extrinsic work values. *Career Development Quarterly*, *58*(3), 276–287. https://doi.
   org/10.1002/j.2161-0045.2010.tb00193.x

Locmele-Lunova, R., & Cirjevskis, A. (2017). Exploring the multigenerational workforce's personal and work values: The future research agenda. *Journal of Business
   Management*, *13*(1/2), 7–19.

Mitchell, T. R., Holtom, B. C., Lee, T. W. & Erez, M. (2001). Why people stay: Using job
   embeddedness to predict voluntary turnover. *Academy of Management Journal*,
   44(6), 1102–1122. https://doi.org/10.5465/3069391

Poehnell, G., & Amundson, N. (2001). *Career crossroads: A personal career positioning
   system*. Ergon Communications.

Schein, E. H. (1992). Career anchors and job/role planning: The links between career
   planning and career development. In D. H. Montross & C. J. Shinkman (Eds.),
   Career development: Theory and practice. C.C. Thomas.

Schwartz, S. H., Cieciuch, J., Vecchione, M., Davidov, E., Fischer, R., Beierlein, C., & Konty, M. (2012). Refining the theory of basic individual values. *Journal of Personality and Social Psychology, 103*(4), 663–688. https://doi.org/10.1037/a0029393

Super, D. E. & Sverko, B. (1995). Life roles, values, and careers: International findings of the Work Importance Study. Jossey-Bass.

Wohrmann, A. M., Fasbender, U., & Deller, J. (2016). Using work values to predict post-retirement work intentions. *Career Development Quarterly, 64*(2), 98–113. https://doi.org/10.1002/cdq.12044

CONNECTING WITH OTHERS: SOCIAL, EMOTIONAL, AND FINANCIAL SUPPORT

OBJECTIVES

This chapter focuses on important sources of support. After reading and completing activities in this chapter, you will be able to do the following:

- Access your allies to support your career-life goals

- Acknowledge the influences of culture, community, attitude, and expectations

- Access mentors, coaches, and guides to help you continue to grow

- Find like-minded people

- Be strategic about your style to manage the impression others form of you

- Recognize the influence of financial management on achieving career-life goals

- Strengthen your supports

CASE EXAMPLE

Sam was enjoying work as a certified professional accountant. After 10 years in the field, the work continued to be fascinating, income was good, and the hours generally worked well with Sam's other role as the single parent of an active 6-year-old child, Izzy. Sam's employer was family friendly and the out-of-school care center was right at the school and permitted drop-offs as early as 7 a.m. and pick-ups until 6 p.m.; it also covered professional development days and school holidays, including winter break, spring break, and summer.

Although single parenting had many challenges, Sam had a good support network that included neighbors, parents of Izzy's school friends, Izzy's grandfather, and a subscription to an on-call nanny network. Sam also had other professional supports in place including a counselor, yoga classes, and tutoring for Izzy. Izzy was enrolled in several sports activities, and Sam and Izzy enjoyed camping in their trailer on many spring and summer weekends. Every summer they looked forward to a flight to visit Izzy's godparents who lived about 4 hours away, across an international border.

Life was going reasonably smoothly until the pandemic changed everything. When schools closed for spring break, the out-of-school care was still open. Sam's office closed but work continued, with Sam expected to put in a full 8-hour day at home. However, the next day, the out-of-school care center closed and people were told to self-isolate and "stay home." Sam was proud of the townhouse they lived in, but its open-concept design didn't offer much privacy for the numerous Zoom meetings and phone calls that kept Sam in touch with colleagues and clients. Nor did it offer much space for a 6-year-old to run off excess energy. To keep their sanity, Sam and Izzy took their dogs out often for walks and went on bike rides with friends. When spring break ended, Sam was expected to add homeschooling Izzy to a life that was already overloaded. Parks were closed, so camping trips were cancelled—trips that had been a stabilizing factor for Sam's mental health. The nanny service closed due to the need for social distancing and self-isolation and, as older people were considered most vulnerable, they stopped seeing Izzy's grandfather who had also been a back-up babysitter in past emergencies. Sam's work was disrupted and productivity suffered. Sam considered quitting what had, until a couple week's earlier, been a dream job.

Although single parents, like Sam, face unique career and life challenges, everybody needs support. Despite the tendency of Western cultures to prize independence and autonomy, people have historically thrived in interdependent communities, and many cultures today are grounded in collectivist values. In countless ways, resources and other people will impact your career success and your sense of satisfaction with work and other life roles. In this chapter, the focus will be on identifying and accessing practical sources of support that will help you to establish and maintain a successful, fulfilling career. Identifying these supports is the final step in the self-clarity stage of the Hope-Action Theory. Your supports will also help to bolster your sense of hope as you recognize that you're not alone on your career journey.

Access Your Allies to Support Your Career-Life Goals

Canadian career development specialists identified five underlying principles that are foundational to many career resources. These principles generally are referred to as the "High Five":

- Know yourself, believe in yourself, and follow your heart

- Change is constant

- Learning is ongoing

- Focus on the journey

- Access your allies

The principle "access your allies" acknowledges that successful people do not get through life alone. Allies are helpful to you at each stage of your career planning and development. They can do the following:

- Share insights about specific occupations, organizations, and professional development opportunities

- Provide an insider's perspective about careers/workplaces you are considering (and your "fit")

- Open your eyes to career possibilities that you may not otherwise have considered

- Open doors by introducing you to others in their networks

- Share tips about parenting, professional etiquette, preparing for interviews, and settling into an occupation or specific workplace

- Serve as mentors, sharing insights and tips as your career continues to develop

- Comfort you in times of disappointment

- Celebrate with you at times of great accomplishment

All of your allies are supportive individuals who have your best interests in mind. However, each may know you from different life arenas (e.g., home, community, school, church, sports) and therefore have different perspectives on your strengths and potential barriers. No one will know you as well as you know yourself. Despite this limitation, your allies can help reduce some of your blind spots, emphasize some of your extraordinary talents, and, in some cases, provide clear and gentle feedback about areas you may need to improve or further develop in order to accomplish your goals.

Tip Learn to appropriately weigh advice you receive—and consider the source.

Supportive people in your life are committed to helping you; however, in most cases, they don't know what help you need. As you connect to ask for feedback or guidance, take the opportunity to update them on your career aspirations and progress. This type of networking may even generate job leads.

Not all supportive individuals in your life can or will make equal contributions. For example, a family friend who is the CEO of a company may intimately know industry trends and corporate strategy but have no understanding at all of your talents or personal style and no sense of the realities of entry-level work in the sector. Sports teammates, on the other hand, may know your style well and have a good understanding of how you'd fit in the workplace. They may also be helpful in coaching you about current interview practices. However, they may not have an accurate "big picture" perspective of how the global economy impacts an organization's strategic direction.

ACTIVITY 8.1 *Self-Clarity Themes*

Reflect on insights you've gained through "accessing your allies" and from any assessment activities you have completed. Use the space provided to note patterns and themes (e.g., did 8 out of 10 people comment on your people skills? Your attention to detail? Your positive attitude?). For example, Sam's themes include perseverance and conscientiousness.

Sample: Sam's Self-Clarity Themes

THEME	SOURCES AND COMMENTS
Perseverance	Employer, counselor, Izzy's godfather, and personality assessment
Conscientiousness	Accounting clients, Izzy's friends' parents, Izzy's grandfather

Now it's your turn; complete the following table.

Self-Clarity Themes

THEME	SOURCES AND COMMENTS

Some of the feedback from others, however, may be a bit confusing. There may be inconsistencies (e.g., One person said you were always positive; two others said that you seemed very serious and "down" most of the time). There may also be a pattern of responses that differ from your own perception of yourself. Reflect on the relationship you have with the people who provided contradictory feedback (e.g., Does one know you from work, perhaps on a project you're struggling in? Does the other know you from family events?). The following activity will help you learn from contradictory information.

ACTIVITY 8.2 *Learning From Contradictions*

Use the following table to record three to five puzzling contradictions from the feedback you've received from others and/or self-assessment activities. Identify the sources of the contradictory feedback and make brief notes to clarify these contradictions. For example, Sam noticed that friends noted attributes like outgoing and energetic, but the counselor noted a tendency to tire easily and a need for some time off:

Sample: Sam's Learning From Contradictions Table

CONTRADICTIONS	SOURCES AND COMMENTS
Outgoing and energetic versus tire easily/need for time off	Friends Counselor—hears the full story, unfiltered Notes: When I pace myself and engage in self-care, I have the energy to do a good job at work and as a single parent

Now it's your turn; complete the following table.

Learning from Contradictions

CONTRADICTIONS	SOURCES AND COMMENTS

ACTIVITY 8.3 *Integrating Feedback With the Work That Interests You*

To help you clarify your career goals, consider the differences between the feedback you are getting and your understanding of the requirements for work that interests you. Use the spaces provided to reflect on the following questions:

In what types of situations are you most relaxed and comfortable?

_____

_____

What do you struggle with?

_____

_____

What characteristics do people from different parts of your life recognize or comment on? For example, do your colleagues see your leadership qualities and your employers see your attention to detail?

_____

_____

Do you have to make any changes to your career goals to realistically align them with your personal style and strengths and the current context of your life?

_____

_____

Hope is at the center of the Hope-Action Theory. Reflect on Activities 8.1 to 8.3. Describe how self-clarity—having a clearer understanding of who you are and what you have to contribute—enhances your confidence in your career plans and life goals.

_____

_____

The Influences of Culture, Community, Attitude, and Expectations

Ironically, some of the most supportive people in your life—family members, employers, coaches, or close friends—may not be supportive in terms of your career planning or development; it's important to cautiously evaluate all the advice you may get. For example, parents may have their own expectations for your career; friends may want to keep you nearby; and coaches may not want to lose a star player. Spouses may have concerns about money, time, or relocation. Although it's important to have significant relationships, they can definitely complicate career decisions.

Some of the influential voices you hear may actually be from the past; you may be carrying messages in your head from previous interactions with important people in your life. Perhaps you promised a dying grandparent that you would go to college to become a lawyer. Or, conversely, perhaps an abusive parent relentlessly told you that you'd never amount to anything. Perhaps a coach, just before retirement, told you that you were the best pitcher he'd ever seen and that you'd be crazy not to continue with a professional career in baseball. Sometimes these voices (even the negative ones) serve as inspiring motivators. However, other times they imprison you. Voices from the past are hard to argue with, even if you now have new information to dispute them. It may be important to access other allies, perhaps even professional counselors, to help you integrate truths from old messages with the reality of who you are today.

ACTIVITY 8.4 *Voices From the Past*

Use the following table to identify the voices from your past that may be influencing your career planning today (e.g., Sam's mother had always said that "our family can support itself—we don't need help from the government").

Sample: Sam's Voices From the Past Table

WHO	MESSAGE	IMPLICATION
Mom	Don't take financial help from government	Because of the pandemic, there are several emergency programs to help compensate for lost wages, to pay for childcare, or to defer rent and loan payments. If I access them, I'll be disappointing my mother.

Now it's your turn; complete the following table.

Voices From the Past

WHO	MESSAGE	IMPLICATION

The roots of some messages go much deeper than the messenger; everyone is a member of several cultural groups, and members of each of those groups share some common beliefs and expectations. Today's understanding of culture goes far beyond ethnicity (although your ethnic background may well be one of your cultural influences). Also, consider your spiritual beliefs, gender, sexual orientation, age, nationality, socioeconomic status, geographic location—really, any contextual factors that may have shaped your beliefs and expectations. As you complete the following activity, reflect on cultural traditions that have influenced you (e.g., Are important decisions made independently, discussed with the family, or made only after consultation with elders or spiritual advisors?). Who will you involve in your career decision?

ACTIVITY 8.5 *The Impact of Culture*

Use the table provided to identify some of the cultural groups you identify with and the messages about career that those cultural affiliations have influenced (e.g., Sam's profession is a source of family pride; for others, cultural influences could include immigrant family—education is the key to success—or rural community—limited job opportunities).

Sample: Sam's Impact of Culture Table

CULTURAL GROUP	MESSAGE	IMPLICATION
Family	Accounting is a prestigious profession	Keeping a professional job is important; quitting work or cutting back would be perceived as failure

Now it's your turn; complete the following table.

The Impact of Culture

CULTURAL GROUP	MESSAGE	IMPLICATION

CULTURAL GROUP	MESSAGE	IMPLICATION

A specific subculture is your immediate family. If you are in a committed relationship, it can be complicated to juggle two careers concurrently. Dual career couples often find it challenging to decide whose career will come first at career crossroads. For example, if one gets an amazing job offer that requires relocation, is the other prepared to give up a great job? If one has to work overtime to meet a deadline, will the other be able to arrange to pick children up from daycare?

In Sam's case, however, the sole responsibility for supporting the family financially and taking care of household responsibilities and chilcare resides in one person. What happens when professional work deadlines and a lack of childcare options collide?

ACTIVITY 8.6 *The Impact of Relationships on Careers*

If you are in a committed relationship, or expect to be in one as your career develops, use the space provided to consider how this may impact the career you are considering and, in turn, how that type of career may impact your relationship. Keep in mind that committed relationships extend beyond romantic partnerships. For example, Sam has sole responsibility for a young child and is also concerned about an aging father. This has an impact on the hours Sam can work and the geographic location of that work.

_____

_____

_____

_____

_____

_____

_____

Tip Optimism is linked to career success and job satisfaction. A positive attitude and a spirit of hopefulness can significantly impact your career development.

As we've discussed throughout this book, hope is at the center of the Hope-Action Theory. In previous research, optimism was discovered to be the single best predictor of both career success and job satisfaction (Neault, 2002). Optimistic people are resilient. One dictionary definition of resilience is "cheerful buoyancy"—what a great fit for Hope-Action Theory! Optimistic people tend to have faith in the future, a sense that things will work out. They tend to believe in their industry and organization; they also believe in themselves.

ACTIVITY 8.7 *Hope for the Future*

A positive attitude makes a very important contribution to personal development. Lack of hope, on the other hand, can unnecessarily restrict career opportunities. Without hope, you may not strive for advanced education or a more challenging job. Use the space provided to reflect on what you hope for in the next stages of your career-life journey. For example, Sam hopes to find better options for working from home while taking care of Izzy

_____

_____

_____

_____

_____

_____

_____

Employers also value a positive attitude. In countless surveys, employers emphasize "soft skills" as essential to career success. Such attributes include interpersonal skills (getting along with people), initiative (being proactive), adaptability (changing direction or making adjustments when necessary), diligence (getting the job done), creativity (thinking of new approaches or solutions), and honesty. However, near the top of most employer survey results is an enthusiastic, positive attitude. Employers want staff and managers who bring positive energy to the workplace—people who are engaging and inspiring.

ACTIVITY 8.8 *Staying Positive at Work*

Use the space provided in the table to identify 10 ways to keep your attitude positive. For each, identify a tangible way to demonstrate your positive attitude at work. For example, Sam realizes that finding adequate childcare for Izzy until school and out-of-school care are both reopened is essential for staying positive during the day.

Sample: Sam's Staying Positive at Work Table

STRATEGIES FOR STAYING POSITIVE	EVIDENCE IN THE WORKPLACE
Arranging temporary childcare	Energetic contributions, enthusiasm, clear thinking, meeting deadlines

Now it's your turn; complete the following table.

Staying Positive at Work

	STRATEGIES FOR STAYING POSITIVE	EVIDENCE IN THE WORKPLACE
1		
2		
3		
4		
5		
6		
7		
8		
9		
10		

Despite your best intentions, it can be hard to stay positive when your expectations collide with the workplace reality. It's frustrating to be hired for your education and experience but then be expected to do mundane tasks at work. It's disappointing to be promised a promotion but have it put on hold due to changes in the economy or because the person you were to replace decided not to retire when expected. It's discouraging, especially when you always got great marks at school, to try your very best at work but constantly get feedback that your best simply isn't good enough. The

COVID-19 pandemic caught the whole world by surprise—many people found it hard to remain positive when the future seemed so uncertain, especially if, financially, they were no longer able to pay all of their bills.

Achieving and sustaining career success requires managing your attitude and expectations. Keep your destination in mind and make the small daily adjustments necessary to keep your attitude upbeat and your expectations aligned with the realities of the workplace and the local and global economies. Victor Frankl (1984), under the toughest of circumstances while he was in a Nazi prison in World War II, reflected on "the last of the human freedoms—to choose one's attitude in any given set of circumstances, to choose one's own way" (p. 86). You, too, can choose your attitude as you continue on your career journey. Sometimes, you'll need support from mentors, coaches, or guides to keep your attitude positive and your journey on track. The next section discusses the supports that people like these can offer.

Access Mentors, Coaches, and Guides to Help You Continue to Grow

The terms *mentors, coaches*, and *guides* are sometimes used interchangeably. Here, however, *mentors* are generally helpful to your career development but aren't positioned to provide specific coaching or skill development. You may have formal or informal relationships with your mentors (e.g., you may be formally assigned a mentor through a program at school or through a professional association, or you may informally ask an acquaintance to be your mentor). In some cases, the relationship may be so informal that the mentor isn't even aware of serving in that role; an example would be a leader in the field you are watching from afar. You can learn a lot from a mentor through observation, research (finding his or her resume or bio online), and benchmarking (comparing your current level of skills and experience to the level the mentor has achieved to be successful).

ACTIVITY 8.9 *Identify Potential Mentors*

The next three steps will help you identify individuals who would be suitable candidates for the role of mentor and who could contribute to your career success.

1. Take a moment to identify the characteristics you would like in a mentor such as good listener, expert at _____, connected to _____ industry, and so on.

---

2. Next, identify sources for potential mentors such as college mentorship programs, professional associations, and so on.

3. Finally, if you already have a mentor in mind, write down the name and set some specific goals to work on with your mentor's support.

1. Mentor characteristics

_____

_____

_____

2. Potential sources of mentors

_____

_____

_____

3. Specific possibilities and goals to work on together

_____

_____

_____

ACTIVITY 8.10 *Identify Potential Coaches*

The term *coach* is used here to describe a slightly different role than a mentor. Generally, coaches have the opportunity to observe you in action and provide specific feedback that will help you develop work-related skills and attitudes. Use the space in the table to identify three specific skills that a coach might be able to help you with.

Beside each, identify who might be able to coach you (consider friends, colleagues, instructors, supervisors, or other trusted allies). To get you started, an example is completed for Sam.

Sample: Sam's Identify Potential Coaches Table

SKILL OR ATTITUDE	POTENTIAL COACH
Time-management skills, meeting deadlines	Cam Smithers, CPA, a home-based accountant

Now it's your turn; complete the following table.

Identify Potential Coaches

SKILL OR ATTITUDE	POTENTIAL COACH

ACTIVITY 8.11 *Accessing Guidance*

Guides, on the other hand, may include anyone who provides you with wisdom and sound advice. Members of some cultural communities consult elders before making big decisions; members of other communities consult spiritual advisors. Parents and older siblings guide many career decisions. In the workplace, leaders of professional associations, speakers, instructors, professors, labor market analysts, economists, authors, and journalists all provide career-related guidance. In the community service and educational systems, career counselors and academic advisors may serve as guides. Use the table to list specific questions you have at this stage of your career journey. Identify two or three potential guides (or sources of guidance) for each of your questions. The example provided relates to Sam's concerns about arranging temporary childcare for Izzy, given the COVID-19-related social distancing and self-isolation mandates.

Sample: Sam's Accessing Guidance Table

QUESTION	POTENTIAL GUIDES/SOURCE OF GUIDANCE
Is there any childcare available for Izzy? / Can I share a nanny with someone?	Check with parents of Izzy's friends, the on-call nanny service, my professional association, colleagues, and family members to see if anyone is available and seems safe to come into our home.

Now it's your turn; complete the following table.

Accessing Guidance

QUESTION	POTENTIAL GUIDES/SOURCE OF GUIDANCE

Strategic Impression Management

Mentors, coaches, and guides may all be useful sources of support as you prepare to create a positive first impression with those who will impact your career progress. Every industry, region, and organization has unwritten rules about "the way things are done around here." Similar to having an instructor or guide advise you about the right equipment for any new adventure, it's important to know how to network effectively, dress appropriately, and speak and write in a way that fits your audience. There isn't a "one-size-fits-all" approach to this, despite the proliferation of articles and self-help books on the topic. As you transition from school to work, between careers, or into increasing responsibilities in your current organization, consider everything that contributes to the first impression others form about you. In the context of career changes related to the pandemic, impression management includes how to maintain a professional image when working from home!

ACTIVITY 8.12 *Impression Management*

Use the following table as you consider changes you may need to make as you prepare for the next stage in your career (e.g., in Sam's case, working from home as a professional accountant). If the item is contributing to a positive impression, put a checkmark in the "recommended change column" and leave as is. If it has the potential to create a negative impression, list a recommended change in the space provided.

ITEM	RECOMMENDED CHANGE
E-mail address	
Voicemail message (landline)	
Voicemail message (mobile)	
Online presence (Facebook)	
Online presence (personal web page)	
Online presence (other)	
Background and lighting for teleconferences (e.g., Zoom)	
Microphone and speakers for teleconferences (e.g., Zoom)	
Hair (cut, color)	
Fingernails (and toenails if wearing open-toed shoes)	

ITEM	RECOMMENDED CHANGE
Clothing (**Tip** Aim to dress for the position one level above the one you are applying for)	
Shoes	
Outerwear	
Level of language	
Spelling/grammar	
E-mail abbreviations (**Tip** Reserve casual abbreviations such as TTFN, LOL, or ROFL for family and friends)	
Etiquette (formality, manners, appropriate follow-up)	

Keep in mind that "impression management" is not about creating a fake persona. We all have different types of clothes in our closet that we wear for specific purposes. Impression management is simply about being intentional—choosing when and for which purpose to share different aspects of ourselves.

In the case of some career considerations such as disability or, in Sam's case, single parenting, it will be important to decide if, when, or how to disclose. Strategic disclosure—giving adequate information to the people who need it—is important; mentors, coaches, or guides may be helpful in developing a disclosure strategy. Culture audits, which involve observing potential organizations in person or online to detect their diversity, may be useful in determining how to approach disclosure. In some cases, letting a potential or new employer know about a disability or other career consideration is required in order to arrange accommodations. For example, Sam may temporarily need a shorter work week or the opportunity to take extra time off until childcare becomes available again. However, sometimes early disclosure may lead to real or perceived discrimination: If Sam had discussed being a single parent during an interview and then didn't get the job simply due to not being the most qualified candidate, it might appear that the hiring decision had discriminated based on family status. However, choosing not to disclose could result in misunderstandings after being hired if it became apparent that Sam was unable to manage the everyday demands of the job to the same extent as other employees.

The Influence of Financial Management on Achieving Career-Life Goals

Career transitions may require extra financial support upfront and, especially in the case of post-graduation careers or promotions, may bring with them a significant increase in financial resources. If you acquired student loans while preparing for your career, be sure you are completely familiar with repayment requirements and options. If you have debt from multiple sources, such as credit cards or car loans, consider speaking with your banker about a consolidation loan to organize your finances more efficiently and, in some cases, reduce your interest payments. In the context of the COVID-19 pandemic, governments in various parts of the world were offering emergency loans and banks and creditors were offering payment deferrals. However, such supports, although they are welcome in the short term, can exacerbate longer term financial challenges.

As you prepare for your next job search or make decisions about your current work situation, carefully distinguish between wants and needs. For example, you may *need* an outfit for interviews and networking events; you may *want* something new with a designer label and may *not want* to wear the same outfit to several different events. Chances are, your contacts will not notice that you've worn the same basic outfit more than once as long as it's appropriate and it looks neat and clean.

Some job searching may require some investment in travel as well, whether local (resulting in increased fuel or transit costs) or farther afield (requiring flights and accommodation). Look ahead and begin to save, or find a viable source of support, for such expenses. In the COVID-19 context, job opportunities may be postponed and/or hiring decisions delayed. Individuals who have a bit of an emergency fund in their savings account are better able to navigate such unexpected events.

ACTIVITY 8.13 *Work-Related Expenses*

Use the space provided in the table to jot down your anticipated expenses related to getting or keeping work, starting a business, juggling "gig" work, being unemployed, or graduating and transitioning to the workforce. Consider where money will come from to cover those costs. For example, Sam needed extra money to hire a nanny when the out-of-school center closed during the social distancing phase of the COVID-19 pandemic.

Sample: Sam's Work-Related Expenses Table

ITEM	COST	SOURCE OF $
Nanny	$500/week	Government subsidy—$150/week Grandfather—$150/week Savings—$100/week Normal babysitting budget—$100/week

Now it's your turn; complete the following table.

Job Search/Post-Graduation Expenses

ITEM	COST	SOURCE OF $

Once you've secured the position of your dreams, be strategic about allocating salary increases; if you have become used to living on less, a new job or promotion can offer a great opportunity to pay down debts or add to savings.

Strengthening Your Supports

Whether for social, emotional, or financial support, most people rely on others. As previously discussed, strategic networking can help to build and sustain the supports you'll need. Sometimes, however, you'll need supports beyond what your networks can offer; don't overlook the myriad of community agencies and organizations that can offer practical support when you need it.

Depending on your need for support, consider joining associations (community based or professional) or support groups. There's often a synergy in groups, where the whole becomes significantly stronger than the sum of its individual parts.

It's important to acknowledge that your need for learning will be life-long; that is, your education isn't "done" when you graduate. Therefore, as you expand your sources of support, consider what future education or training you might need to sustain your career success.

Summary

In the opening case example and through many of the activities, we shared Sam's story. Sam had achieved success as an accountant and had carefully constructed a life that worked as a single parent to Izzy, a 6-year-old child. However, that careful construction collapsed in the aftermath of the COVID-19 pandemic when Sam was expected to work from home, homeschool Izzy, and isolate from Izzy's grandfather, school, out-of-school care, friends, and family. Sam needed to set up new supports during this temporary crisis, maintain virtual contact with other supports, and juggle finances to cope with a new reality. Just like Sam, you, too, will need supports—we all do!

This chapter has provided information about accessing your allies and soliciting feedback from those who know you well. You have considered the impact of culture, community, attitude, and expectations. You were encouraged to consider who might serve as mentors, coaches, and guides as you continue your career journey to seek out like-minded people and to reflect on the importance of impression management and financial management.

As the chapter concluded, the emphasis was on expanding your supports and committing to lifelong learning. Use the questions in the next section to reflect on your learning from this chapter and take it to a deeper level through discussion. Within Hope-Action Theory, after you get clear about who you are and what you'll need to succeed, the next stages include visioning, goal setting, and planning. With self-clarity and supports in place, you are ready to move on to envisioning, and planning for, a career path that fits you.

Questions for Reflection and Discussion

1. Reflect on Sam's story, shared in the opening case example. What kinds of supports may be needed to maintain a successful career during the pandemic? How might such supports be put in place?

   Write down a specific question you have about transitioning from school or unemployment to work. Some examples include, "What do I wear to a Chamber of Commerce networking event? When do I have to start paying back student loans? What professional associations should I join as a [name the occupation]? What is a good local source of high-quality, inexpensive, business casual clothes? What government grants are available to support me in starting a business?" Identify at least two possible sources of information (e.g., people you already know, specific websites, friends of friends). Check one of those sources to see if you can find your answer. If not, try the second source. If the answer still isn't apparent, consider what other sources might be useful. Reflect on how a similar approach—such as asking specific questions, checking the Internet, and asking people in your existing network to respond—might help as you prepare for the next stage on your career journey.

2. Impression management can be a touchy, and potentially offensive, topic. Consider some of your personal reactions as you contemplated changing aspects of yourself in order to assist others to create a positive first impression of you. Reflect on which aspects of yourself you are prepared to adjust and, perhaps more importantly, which aspects you're not prepared to change. What are the implications in terms of what types of work you will be looking for?

References

Frankl, V. E. (1984). *Man's search for meaning* (3rd ed.). Simon & Schuster.

Neault, R. A. (2002). Thriving in the new millennium: Career management in the changing world of work. *Canadian Journal of Career Development, 1*(1), 11–21.

Additional Resources

Business Management Daily Editors (2018). 7 questions to ask your mentor. *Administrative Professional Today, 44*(9), 5.

> Subscribe to the Admininstrative Professional Today's newsletter for helpful articles with relevant news, skills, and strategies to increase productivity and advance your adminstrative career.

Charity Village (n.d.). *Community and social services.* https://charityvillage.com/cms/organizations/community-and-social-services

> Charity Village provides an alphabetized listing of community and social service agencies. Read more about a variety of charitable and nonprofit organizations across Canada and see what job openings they have.

Employment and Social Development Canada. (n.d.). *Services & information.* https://www.canada.ca/en/employment-social-development.html

> This website provides an overview of employment and financial supports in Canada.

Femke. (2017, March 15). How to ask for constructive feedback. *Medium.* https://medium.com/thoughts-from-femke/how-to-ask-for-constructive-feedback-3312a570f7de

> This article emphasizes the importance of well designed questions and provides three strategies to generate high quality feedback.

Rosenberg McKay, D. (2019, April 11). *Why you should have a mentor.* http://career-planning.about.com/od/workplacesurvival/a/mentor.htm

> This website elaborates on the significant impact a mentor could have on your career success.

U.S. Department of Labor. (n.d.). *Agencies and programs.* https://www.dol.gov/general/dol-agencies

> This website provides a listing of the employment and financial supports in the US.

Congratulations! If you have invested the time in reading the information we have provided and working through the activities we have offered, then you now have the information you need for visioning a future you will find meaningful and exciting. (If you have moved too quickly through Section II, then consider redoubling your efforts to do more thorough and in-depth self-reflection, which will lead to stronger self-clarity.)

Using self-clarity, Section III guides you through creating a vision of future possibilities that you find meaningful to pursue. This approach contains time-tested and evidence-based practices for helping you get where you hope to be in your life. Once you have developed a vision, you need to translate that into specific goals. Such goals become guideposts for moving forward in positive ways that you find meaningful and purposeful. If goals represent guideposts on this part of the journey, then plans represent a more specific road map for moving toward your desired destination. Goals and plans must often be revised as you acquire new information about yourself and the world. Thus, all goals and plans are somewhat tentative while at the same time being tied to what you know about yourself and the world thus far.

VISIONING, GOAL SETTING, AND PLANNING

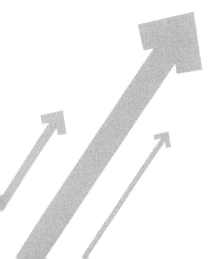

9 VISIONING FUTURE POSSIBILITIES

OBJECTIVES

This chapter introduces you to the importance of visioning future possibilities for your career. After reading and completing activities in this chapter, you will be able to do the following:

- Learn how to engage in visioning
- Be able to apply the concept of flow as it relates to your career development
- Increase the probability of career flow occurring in your life
- Understand the importance of vision statement
- Engage in brainstorming to create a vision of future career possibilities.
- Create a personal vision statement

CASE EXAMPLE

In Daryll's most recent job, he was an events planner for a large hotel chain. Daryll loved the work he did. Although it was often challenging, Daryll always had a strong sense of commitment to ensuring that any event he helps plan goes off as perfectly as possible. From an early age, he can remember planning and organizing activities. His friends relied upon him to "make things happen". He has always "just been that way." So, when he lost his job due to the pandemic, it left him feeling confused and uncertain.

Daryll had many questions. He wondered whether his unemployment was going to be long-term, permanent, or temporary. Should he retrain? Wait it out?

He simply was unsure what to do. As he considered the future, it seemed just as unclear. Prior to losing his job, he thought he knew what he wanted for his future. Now, he wasn't so sure. He doubted everything, but mostly himself. Imagining the future seemed like an impossible task.

Daryll was clear about what he enjoyed in his work. And he still enjoyed traveling and visiting new places. He also enjoyed helping others. Maybe what he needed most of all right now was some reassurance and help moving forward.

Visioning

Visioning involves identifying desired future scenarios and brainstorming future possibilities. Put another way, it involves clarifying what you hope most for in your life and translating these hopes into your personal vision statement. Some argue that this activity is unrealistic. We say, they're right! However, if you are not able to envision your most desired future state, your chances of getting anywhere close to that state is severely limited. There is always room for compromise in life, but why start there? Visioning future possibilities is a creative and fun activity that leads to identifying goals that capture your energy and excitement. Often, however, people need assistance as they create a future vision based on self-clarity. Too many times people only use "probability thinking" to inform their thinking. That is, they are unduly influenced by what others say they can or should do. Do not make that mistake! While the opinions of valued others in your life may be important, those opinions should be just one factor in your decision making. People who are reluctant to consider the most exciting future possibilities often have limiting self-beliefs that sabotage the process of creating a vision of what your future could be like. Some people think that the future must be like the past, including those things about the past they found unsatisfying. Such people adhere to what psychologists who study optimism refer to as a "fixed mind-set." They believe that the past will be the future. They tend to think that competencies cannot be improved. They often avoid taking on challenges and tasks because they fear failure. Fortunately, everyone fails! It is called being human. We all experience outcomes that we wish were different; however, even these outcomes benefit us. We can learn important lessons from all life experiences. Whenever possible, shift your focus from success/failure to learning. Understanding what you are learning as a result of any action you take and then how you can use what you learn to move forward is a much more reasonable approach to the choices we implement.

You may know the story of Michael Jordan, the famous basketball player. As a high school sophomore, Jordan was cut from his high school team. Certainly, this was an outcome that he would have preferred not experiencing at the time. Jordan could have decided that his ability in basketball was fixed and that he would not be able to improve his skills sufficiently to make his high school varsity basketball team. That certainly would have been "probability thinking" in this instance. That is, based on the external information, the probability was that he was not ever going to be a good basketball player. He was not even good enough to make his high school basketball team! Rather than using a fixed mind-set, however, Jordan had a "growth mind-set." He firmly believed that through hard work and discipline he could become a better basketball player. And he loved playing basketball! So rather than becoming a kid who quit playing basketball in his sophomore year of high school because he was not good enough, Jordan developed a goal and strategies for achieving his goal—and went on to become the person many consider to be the best basketball player in history. One of the exciting things about the future is that it has yet to occur.

Future scenarios should be developed free of unnecessary limitations. They should be guided by your self-clarity with minimal input from the "yes, but ..." perspective. To put it another way, future scenarios should not be guided by the reasons you cannot do something. For example, if you love music, are a reasonably accomplished musician, enjoy interacting with other musicians, and find spending time playing music to be especially meaningful, you might envision yourself as a professional musician. The fact that the percentage of musicians who are able to become professional is very small should not, at this point, be considered (that would be probability thinking). Possibility thinking leads you to create as many desirable future scenarios as possible based on your self-clarity; this is the goal of visioning.

Consider the following questions: Do you avoid tasks because of fear of failure? Do you put less effort into tasks because you feel hopeless about making progress? Do you miss learning opportunities because of fear of failure? If you answered yes to any of these questions then you probably do possess the belief that your potential is fixed. There is, however, hope. Studies have shown that we can change our mind-set. To begin this process, you may find it helpful to read about people who have experienced great things. Notice their orientation to thinking about themselves and the future. Consider how you can revise your thinking to increase your orientation to more of a growth mind-set. One way to do this is to identify activities you enjoy doing the most—activities that seem to capture your full attention and in which, when you are fully engaged in them, lead you to performing at your best, when you are in the "flow."

Career Flow

The term *flow* comes from the work of a leading psychologist by the name of Mihaly Csikszentmihalyi. Csikszentmihalyi coined the term *flow* after interviewing a large number of people in an attempt to understand their experience of being totally immersed in an activity—"in the zone," as they say. He found clear patterns among people who experience being in the flow. Learning about these patterns can help people focus their activities in ways that can increase the possibility of having a flow experience, something most people describe as highly desirable.

Because in this book we focus on career planning, we use the term *career flow* to describe the experience of being totally immersed in a work-related activity. By focusing on career flow in your life, you can identify the work activities that you are most likely to find highly satisfying. Although no job is highly satisfying 100% of the time, it makes sense to make educational and career plans that direct you toward an occupation that will be very enjoyable *most* of the time, one that will provide the greatest possibility for experiencing career flow.

Drawing on the work of Csikszentmihalyi, you increase the likelihood of experiencing career flow by participating in work tasks that you find meaningful and appropriately challenging. Additionally, there must be clear goals for the task, and you must receive accurate feedback regarding your task performance. It is important to note that career flow is task specific. Each occupation requires a person to perform a wide variety of tasks. Some tasks will be more desirable than others. In our jobs as university professors, for example, we may experience career flow as we write the chapters of this book but not when we serve on a committee on which we reluctantly agreed to serve. Both tasks, however, are part of our jobs as university professors. It is the specific task that we are engaged in that makes the difference relative to our opportunities to experience career flow.

An important aspect of career flow relates to the challenge level of a task. If the challenge of the task is too great for your skill level, you will feel overwhelmed. If you find that the challenges involved in completing the task are below your skill level, you will become bored with the task. Thus, the challenge of the task must be significant but not beyond your capacity to complete the task successfully.

When asked to describe how they feel when they experience career flow, interviewees have responded with the following comments:

I had lots of energy!

I was in tune with what I was doing.

Time flew!

I had a sense of belonging.

I had a sense of connectedness.

I experienced a sense of intimacy with the activity.

I felt invigorated.

I felt as though I wanted to share with others.

I felt a sense of passion.

I had a feeling of being in alignment.

I had the sense that this is what life should be about.

I felt connected to something bigger.

I felt that I was bringing myself into my work.

I wasn't thinking, I was just doing or being.

Clearly, people describe very powerful and desirable emotions when they focus on career flow experiences. Interestingly, these descriptions relate to what Csikszentmihalyi found in his research. Specifically, he noted that when experiencing flow people often state that they feel a sense of purpose and passion in their activities. They have a real sense of joy. There often is the feeling that "time flew by" while they were engaged in a specific task. When people experience flow, the have a personal investment in what they are doing and experience a connection with the tasks in which they are engaged.

ACTIVITY 9.1 *Career Flow Assessment*

To learn more about career flow in your life, it will help to pay attention to the emotional experiences you have when you engage in a variety of tasks. By focusing your attention in this way, you can begin to increase your awareness of the types of tasks that tend to be associated with experiencing career flow for you. You can begin this process by considering the following questions:

- Which activities would you choose to engage in if you could engage in any activities you wanted to? Why?

- If you woke up tomorrow and could be doing whatever you wanted to do, what would you be doing?

- How would you spend your time?

- What do you enjoy about these activities?

Increasing the Probability of Career Flow Occurring

Csikszentmihalyi (1988) found that flow experiences tend to occur more at work than in leisure activities. Csikszentmihalyi stated that this finding is not surprising because work life tends to be more structured than leisure. Specifically, in work, there are typically performance goals and performance expectations, and feedback is provided. It is also true that work tends to require concentration and engages a person's skills in task behavior. These are all keys for having career flow experiences.

You might wonder about having career flow experiences if your primary life role excludes work due to being unemployed or if you are in a job you dislike. Regardless of your situation, the good news is that even though career flow tends to happen more in work than nonwork activities, it can occur in a variety of life roles (student, partner, leisure activities, etc.) *if you are intentional about your behavior.* Additionally, identifying the tasks that connect with career flow for you in the present will help you in your career planning for the future. By identifying those tasks that bring you the most satisfaction, you begin the process of identifying important information to include in your career goals.

Tip Focus on what matters most to you.

When you engage in tasks that matter to you, you feel a greater sense that you matter. So, another question to consider related to career flow is "What really matters to you?" It is clear that people are more likely to experience career flow when they do work that requires them to use skills that they enjoy using and that they feel reasonably competent using. When people engage in activities that allow them to use their skills in these ways, they do not spend much time worrying about whether they will perform competently. When people are not focused on whether they are competent at a particular task, they engage in less inner questioning (e.g., Am I good enough? What if I make a mistake?) and their focus shifts from themselves to the activity. They do not worry so much about *how* they are doing; rather, they focus on doing what they already know they can do. Doing what you like and feel competent doing it leads you to experience high levels of satisfaction in your activities.

Because you are more likely to experience career flow when you engage in tasks that reflect what is important to you—or what you value (you might refer back to the values activity you did at the beginning of this book)—increasing the probability of you experiencing career flow requires you to be aware of your values as well as your skills. When your activities connect to your values, you do not spend a lot of time pondering the question "Why am I doing this?" You are in sync with your activities and experience a sense of meaning and purpose in what you are doing.

Conversely, when your answers to the question "Why am I doing this?" do not reflect your values, you experience inner conflict that becomes a significant distraction to your capacity to complete the tasks confronting you. When there is little connection between what you do and what you value, you can even become demoralized and depressed over time. You can easily conclude that what you do does not matter, essentially because it does not matter to you.

When the inevitable challenges arise and you are in a situation that is not consistent with your values, it is very difficult to persevere in that situation. Fortunately, the reverse is also true. When what we do connects with what we value, then it becomes easier to tolerate other challenges in our work situation. Many college students experience this when they compare how they feel in courses that relate to their major versus how they feel when they are enrolled in general education courses that do not connect to their values and interests. In the former, the focus is more likely to be on learning the material being taught. In the latter, the focus is more likely to be on asking the question "Why do I need to learn this material?" Thus, engaging in activities that reflect our values provides an important source of motivation for most people. Even in the latter instances, however, a secondary purpose—I am learning this material because it is necessary for me to do so in order to study my major—may be enough to pull you through.

To experience career flow in work it is important, whenever possible, to seek employment opportunities that allow you to do what you enjoy and feel competent doing. When these criteria are met, you are then more likely to experience career flow. You are more likely to find yourself noting that you feel passionate about your work, have an intimate connection with what you do, experience high energy levels, and feel as if time flies by. If not all the time, perhaps some or even most of the time.

ACTIVITY 9.2 *Daryll's Career Flow*

Consider Daryll, the case example provided at the beginning of the chapter. Do you think Daryll experienced career flow as an events planner?

- What factors in Daryll's situation do you think might contribute to his experiencing career flow?

- What factors do you think might make experiencing career flow less likely to occur for Daryll?

- What values was Daryll expressing as an events planner?

- What skills was he using most often?

Now consider your own situation by completing the following activity.

ACTIVITY 9.3 *Your Career Flow*

Think of three specific times in your life when you have experienced what you might identify as career flow in your school, leisure, and work activities (try to identify one experience for each activity area). Describe, in detail, each experience. In your description address each of the following questions:

Step A

- What were you doing at the time?

- Who were you with?

- What was the setting?

- What happened (before, during, and after)?

- What were you feeling (physiologically) at the time you had these experiences? (Describe the physical sensations related to career

---

flow experiences; for example, "I felt lighter, more relaxed, and happy.")

- What skills were you using?
- What values were you expressing?
- What interests were you expressing?

Step B

Take the information identified in Step A and write a one-paragraph statement in which you fill in the blanks in the following sentence:

In my career flow experiences, I most often use the skills of

_____ and express the values of _____. Other

things I notice as being important to me in these moments are

_____.

Step C

Now examine the contexts of your career flow experiences. Identify which activities were solitary activities and which involved others. For the latter, consider the following questions:

- Were you working as part of a team?
- Which type of activity (solitary or group) do you enjoy more?
- Were you were working indoors or outside?
- Which do you enjoy more (indoor activities or outside activities)?
- Were you working under time pressure to complete the task or did time not matter? Which do you enjoy more (time pressure or no time pressure to complete a task)?

Notice anything else that you think is important about your career flow experiences. Describe these:

Now write an overall summary of your career flow experiences, including the values, skills, and contexts that tend to be involved in these experiences. To do this, simply complete the following:

• In my career flow experiences, I tend to:

To practice focusing on career flow experiences, over the course of the next 2 weeks' pay attention to when you experience career flow in your leisure activities and in your role as a student, friend, and/or worker. Notice the physical sensations that accompany your career flow experiences. Describe these experiences in writing (using a journal). When you have these sensations, make a mental note of what you were doing at the time (better yet, write it down at that point). Keep a journal in which you write daily about your career flow experiences. Describe each moment you had. Reflect on what these moments say about you (your feelings, values, motivations, skills, interests, etc.). Then, in a way similar to what you did in the previous activity, deconstruct what was occurring in those moments and identify the skills, values, interests, and so on that you were expressing at those times. Collectively, these steps help you to develop self-clarity regarding your career flow experiences.

The career flow exercises are important. They are your clues to the sort of activities you may want to engage in more frequently. When you increase your participation in activities that draw on the competencies you enjoy using and that allow you to express your most valued values, you often have reactions similar to those mentioned earlier regarding career flow (e.g., "I feel a sense of passion," "I have a feeling of being in alignment," "I have the sense that this is what life should be about," "I feel natural and genuine"). In other words, you are engaging in the sort of experiences that most likely are desirable and fulfilling for you. These experiences are essential for envisioning your future.

Brainstorming Future Possibilities

Developing a growth mind-set and being clear about activities in which you are most likely to experience flow are critical to successful visioning. In visioning you use the strategy of brainstorming to identify desired possibilities for your future. Brainstorming involves identifying creative solutions to specific problems or questions. It is something that can be done in groups or individually. Individuals engage in brainstorming for reasons such as identifying a career goal, resolving a relationship issue, selecting a specific option from a group of options, and so on.

There are specific guidelines that are important to follow in order to brainstorm possible career futures effectively. First, brainstorming focuses on quantity not quality. The goal is to devise a list of career options that is as expansive as possible. No idea is stupid. No idea is bad. Do not take time to engage in self-criticism or dismiss any idea prematurely. Generate as many options as you can. Second, limit the time you set aside for brainstorming. If possible, set a timer. Typically, 10–15 minutes should be sufficient. Whatever time frame you select, stick to it and make it relatively brief. Limiting your time helps you focus on developing the *quantity* of your list. Third, write down the ideas you generate. You can use Post-it notes, for example, and write one idea on each Post-it note. See how many Post-it notes you can use.

> **Tip** In brainstorming, the only bad idea is the one that is not expressed.

Begin by reviewing your career flow experiences. Read them over several times. After reading them several times, imagine yourself engaging in several of your career flow experiences. Taking one experience at a time, imagine yourself engaging in a career flow experience. Once you have visualized yourself engaging in several career flow activities, complete the Activity 9.4.

ACTIVITY 9.4 *Brainstorming Activity*

In the next 5 minutes, complete the sentence that follows as many times as possible. Write each idea down (ideally on a Post-it note). Keep your responses brief. Do not limit yourself to actual jobs. Incorporate as many aspects of yourself as possible. Have some fun and combine activities into a job that you create yourself.

- My dream job is:

Once you are done, take a few moments to notice how you feel and what your energy level is. Are you energized? Because you have been focusing on using your creativity to identify possible futures that incorporate your career flow experiences, there is a good chance that you feel rather positive and energetic right now. Perhaps you are even excited about some of the possibilities you identified. Make a mental note of your reactions. These positive reactions serve as signposts that direct you to activities that will increase your career flow experiences.

Review the possibilities you generated and select three that seem of most interest to you. Examine these possibilities with an eye toward identifying themes that they have in common with each other. For example, Daryll may have themes related to creating opportunities for others to celebrate important moments in their lives. If so, it might be helpful for him to begin considering how these themes relate to actual jobs. Once you have identified potential occupations of interest, spend some time learning more about them.

Personal Vision Statement Guidelines

Using the themes you identified, you are ready to develop your personal vision statement. A vision statement is a vivid description of your desired future. It is your personal creation of an image that reflects the future you hope to create. It is your dream for yourself. It should be a statement that you find compelling and exciting. It should incorporate the most important aspects of who you are, what you enjoy, the skills you enjoy using, and what you value. You are describing the desired destination for your career flow journey. You are creating a statement than can serve as your guide as you make your educational and career plans. It is your opportunity to dream big dreams!

Before writing your vision statement, it is helpful to review some guidelines for this activity. Your vision statement should be one that describes your ideal future career. It should describe the future you hope to create using a future time frame. Incorporate powerful language to describe a vision that is powerful to you. For example, the vision statement for the organization known as "One Laptop Per Child" is as follows: "To create educational opportunities for the world's poorest children by providing each child with a rugged, low-cost, low-power, connected laptop with content and software designed for collaborative, joyful, self-empowered learning"

(One Laptop per Child, n.d.). This is a powerful statement of great ambition. Notice that the creators of this vision statement did not aspire to provide laptops to many middle-class children or even most children living in economically challenged situations. Their vision is much more powerful than that. They sought to provide laptops for all of the poorest children in the world. The statement is compelling and inspirational.

The purpose of your vision statement is to create a mental picture charged with emotion that can serve to energize and inspire you. Take as much space as you need to accomplish this with your vision statement. Be sure to create a vision statement that describes the best possible future outcome for you. Make your vision statement just as lofty and ambitious as the vision statement created by those involved in the One Laptop Per Child organization. It should describe what you aspire to achieve. Include as much as you can from your career flow experiences.

It is also important to keep in mind that your vision statement is aspirational. In this sense, it is useful as a guide to assess whether your career is flowing in a direction toward your vision. It is not useful as a measuring stick for assessing whether you have been successful in achieving your vision. For example, success for the One Laptop Per Child organization could be operationalized by their having significantly increased the number of poor children with laptops living in developing countries. It would not be reasonable to consider them as being unsuccessful if every child does not have a laptop. In this sense, vision statements are idealistic in that they often are nearly impossible to achieve. They are also realistic, however, because they draw on your core values, interests, skills, and hopes for your future. Thus, they set the course for you to achieve your dreams, and they are a useful tool for stimulating your inspiration, creativity, motivation, and imagination. As Albert Einstein said, "Imagination is more powerful than knowledge." Imagination allows you to see the exciting possibilities for your career. In referring to his brother, Robert F. Kennedy, Jr., the late Senator Edward Kennedy stated at his brother's funeral that "some men see things as they are and say, 'Why?' I dream of things that never were and say, 'Why not?'"

Vision Statement Examples

I will be a better son, brother, sister, student, teammate, co-worker, and friend by being reliable, trustworthy, compassionate, and helpful in all my interactions with others.

I will become an inspirational leader whom people respond to positively because of my vision, creativity, compassion, and excellent work ethic.

I will be a disciplined worker who consistently goes beyond what my boss expects of me, eat only healthy food, and serve as an excellent role model for my coworkers.

I will live each day dedicated to integrity, commitment, challenge, and joy; be a loving daughter and valued friend; travel the world to experience different cultures; and practice my guitar regularly to become an accomplished guitarist.

Now you create your vision statement. We challenge you to make them better than these examples. You can do it!

ACTIVITY 9.5 *Your Personal Vision Statement*

Using the activities and guidelines, construct a vision statement that incorporates what you value the most, what you most enjoy doing, what skills you enjoy using, and what you have always wanted to achieve in your life.

The purpose of the vision statement is to open your eyes to what is *possible*. It should include what brings you happiness, what you enjoy doing, and what you have always wanted to do. When we become aware of what is possible, we begin to realize that dreams can be achieved and that challenges can be overcome. Review your vision statement regularly and use it as a stimulus for engaging in self-reflection as to whether you are on course in your career and educational planning. You may, on occasion, conclude that you need to revise your vision statement to be more in line with your evolving sense of self. Keep focused on the possibilities!

Summary

Visioning involves identifying desired future scenarios and brainstorming future possibilities that embrace your passion and purpose. Visioning involves clarifying what you hope most for in your life and translating these hopes into your personal vision statement. Visioning future possibilities is a creative and fun activity that leads to identifying goals that capture your energy and excitement. Too many times, people only use "probability thinking" to inform their thinking. That is, they are influenced by what others say they can or should do. Some people adhere to what psychologists who study optimism refer to as a "fixed mind-set." They believe that the past will be the future. They tend to think that competencies cannot be improved. They often avoid taking on challenges and tasks because they fear failure. We all experience outcomes that we wish were different; however, even these outcomes benefit us. We can learn important lessons from all life experiences. Whenever possible, shift your focus from success/ failure to learning. Understanding what you are learning as a result of any action you take and then how you can use what you learn to move forward is a much more reasonable approach to the choices we implement.

Questions for Reflection and Discussion

1. Think back over your life and try to recall the various things you wanted to be from the time you were in elementary school to today. Make a list of all the possibilities you have imagined over the course of your life. What do any of them have in common (e.g., helping others, creating something, being in charge, etc.)? How do those themes relate to your personal vision? How are they different? How do you feel about those differences?

2. Make a list of all the times you can recall feeling "in the flow." Consider work and non-work experiences. What interests, values, and skills were you using in each of those moments? Is there a pattern to the list you developed? What does your list suggest about your future possibilities?

References

One Laptop per Child. (n.d.). *Mission statement.* http://laptop.org/en/vision/index.shtml

Csikszentmihalyi, M. (1988). *Optimal experience: Psychological studies of flow in consciousness.* Cambridge University Press.

Additional Resources

A brief description of "flow": http://coe.sdsu.edu/eet/articles/Flowexp/start.htm

Csíkszentmihályi, M. (1990). *Flow: The psychology of optimal experience.* Harper and Row.

TED. (2008, October 24). Mihaly Csikszentmihalyi: Creativity, fulfillment and flow [Video file]. YouTube. https://www.youtube.com/watch?v=fXIeFJCqsPs

GOAL SETTING AND PLANNING 10

OBJECTIVES

This chapter introduces you to strategies and tactics for effective goal setting and planning. After reading and completing activities in this chapter, you will be able to do the following:

- Use a SMART goal-setting strategy

- Set goals that are balanced and relevant to your vision

- Identify and prioritize key action steps toward achieving a goal

- Expect goals and plans to be interrupted and react in a functional way

- Understand the importance of planning, implementing, and adapting when pursuing a goal

CASE EXAMPLE

Jihan is 22 years old and has been working as a facilities management technician at a large automotive company in South Korea for the last 3 years. His production line was shut down for a month during the COVID-19 pandemic; therefore, he started to worry about his long-term future. Unlike the majority of Koreans who go to college right after high school, he started working for the company after graduating from a technical high school. His academic performance was good, but he decided to enter in to the "real world" as he did not think that college education was very practical. When he was a child, he enjoyed creating buildings and objects with Legos and other materials. His role models were inventors such as King Sejong who invented Hangul, the Korean alphabet.

He was somewhat rebellious, especially when what parents and teachers said did not make sense.

At work, he feels energized when solving difficult problems with people, and he has been rewarded for his creativity and engagement. He appreciates the working environment, salary, benefits, and people around him. He realized that he is naturally drawn to influencing the environment where people can feel comfortable and satisfied. His vision is to start a business that facilitates people to thrive in their respective environment exercising control over the environment. He does not have a specific business model or timeline yet. However, he believes that he needs to do two things in order to pursue the vision: (a) understand people and (b) understand the world.

To fulfill his vision, he set six goals. First, he wants to get a bachelor's degree in industrial engineering at a university with tuition assistance from the company. Second, he aims to develop at least one idea for continuous improvement at work. Third, he aims to earn three licenses or certifications related to his work. Fourth, he hopes to become an expat at some point to learn about a new world while working for the company. Fifth, he wants to save at least $50,000 before quitting his job. Sixth, he wants to develop a business model and develop relevant competencies. While pursuing these goals, he is actively looking for ways and key knowledge that will enable him to help people to change in a meaningful direction.

The famous American writer Ralph Waldo Emerson once wrote, "To achieve happiness, we should make certain that we are never without an important goal." A well-designed goal provides a sense of meaning and purpose. The famous professional basketball player Julius Erving noted, "Goals determine what you're going to be." These quotations suggest that being without goals is similar to being adrift at sea and subject to the changing tides and currents. Your destination is unclear. When you have goals, you can use them to set your course, guide your activities, and express your purpose. When you engage in self-reflection, develop self-clarity, and use your self-understanding to envision possible future scenarios, you are ready to identify specific goals for your life. As Gloria Steinem, the American feminist and author, noted, "Without leaps of imagination, or dreaming; we lose the excitement of possibilities. Dreaming, after all, is a form of planning." When you turn your dreams into vision statements, you establish the foundation for identifying goals and then construct plans to achieve your goals.

Effective goal setting can only occur after engaging in crucial foundational work. Hope is essential for developing goals because goals reflect your hope for your future. Goals continue to fuel your hope as you implement plans to move toward the future you hope to create. For example, Martin Luther King, Jr.'s hope for the future fueled his goal of helping to create a more just society. Hope also boosts your ability to persevere when you encounter obstacles to your goals, and having meaningful goals helps you persevere when your hope needs bolstering. The political/civil activist Jesse Jackson is known for encouraging people to "keep hope alive." He knew the necessity for hope when striving toward essential goals.

Hope is essential for goal identification as well as for implementing your plans to achieve your goals. When personal agency beliefs (i.e., when you are confident that if you take specific actions you are likely to achieve meaningful outcomes) combine with taking focused action toward desired goals, then hope exists. Actions occur, however, in an environmental context that also provides feedback relative to goal desirability as well as the probability that you can achieve the goals you have identified. This feedback is an essential aspect of adaptability when you use the new information you acquire as a result of the actions you have taken (e.g., Now that I know what I know, does my identified goal still seem to make sense to me? Is it still desirable? Is it still possible?). These questions lead you back to self-reflection and, subsequently, self-clarity.

Thus, self-reflection and self-clarity are keys to goal development. When you take time to reflect and become clear about what is important to you, what you enjoy, and what you are good at, then you adaptively use this information to envision the possibilities. In this way, self-clarity becomes your anchor to creating your future vision from which you can develop your personal goals. Throughout this entire process, your focus should be on what you are learning as you engage in each step of Hope-Action Theory (HAT) (self-reflection, self-clarity, visioning, goal setting, planning, implementing, and adapting). Thus, your constant partner in these steps is the information you continually acquire from your interactions with your environment. It should be clear that the HAT steps are lifelong as you continue learning more about yourself and your environment.

A SMART Goal-Setting Strategy

This leads us to consider a specific model for establishing personal goals. There are, in fact, many strategies you can use to identify meaningful career goals. A common and useful strategy is referred to by the acronym SMART.

Each letter of the acronym represents essential reminders regarding the goal-setting process. The letter "S" refers to the need to make your goals as specific as possible. Merely having the goal to lose as much weight as possible, for example, is not sufficient. Having the goal of losing 50 pounds to achieve a weight of 200 pounds from the current weight of 250 pounds is more specific.

Similarly, goals must be measurable ("M"). For example, working harder at your studies is not a readily measurable goal compared to the goal of increasing your grades from a C average to a B average. Goals should also be challenging yet achievable ("A"). If a goal is viewed as not achievable (and here is where goals differ from vision statements), then you are not likely to work toward it. If a goal is too easy, then you are not likely to be enthusiastic about pursuing that goal. Thus, goals must be challenging enough to energize you but not so challenging that they lead you to feel hopeless about your chances of achieving them.

Your goals must also be relevant ("R") to your vision that you pictured based on your priorities. Without the relevance of your goal to a bigger picture in your life, it is like building a house on a weak foundation. Another popular understanding of the R in SMART is realistic. Without a specific timeframe ("T") for your goal achievement, it is merely a wish or a dream. By attaching a due date to what you hope to accomplish, you create a temporal sense of how it may progress and a sense of urgency as the deadline approaches. That often propels you to focus and get something done. Let's suppose that you often daydream about playing lead guitar in a touring band, and you just began playing the guitar. Getting into a touring band in the next 6 months would not be a very realistic goal. A more realistic goal that can help you achieve your dream would be to master how to strum the basic chords within the next 2 months, with an ultimate goal to be in a touring band in 2 years.

Note that you should have short-term and long-term goals. Your short-term goals should connect to your long-term goal. For example, a long-term goal could be to lose 50 pounds in the next 5 months to achieve a weight of 200 pounds from your current weight of 250 pounds. Your short-term goal could be to lose 10 pounds this month so that by the end of the month you weigh 240 pounds. Short-term goals help you break your long-term goals into relevant, intentional, and achievable chunks. They help you keep the course so that your behavior stays focused on achieving your long-term goal.

Setting SMART goals is an evolving process. As you begin working toward your goals, you may need to revise them in several ways. For example, you may realize that they are too easy or too difficult or less desirable than you initially thought. You may also need to adjust your timeframe due to unforeseen events. The point is to revisit your goals as you work toward them to make sure that your goals are still SMART for you! Engaging in regular self-reflection increases the likelihood that your goals make sense and remain meaningful to you. Making sure your goals connect to your vision helps you to stay focused on what it is you desire to achieve. Occasionally, it may be useful to take time to visualize your goal. If your goal is to graduate from college with a degree in architecture, for example, imagine seeing yourself walking across the stage at your graduation ceremony, shaking hands with the dean as he or she presents your diploma to you. Imagine yourself in your graduation gown and hat and experience all the positive emotions that accompany this accomplishment. Use this visualization strategy at frequent intervals (it only takes a few minutes, so you may be able to do this three times per week, if not daily). A short-term goal related to your long-term goal could be to increase your study time per day from 30 minutes to 60 minutes, 6 days per week. Be sure to write down your vision statement, long-term goal, and short-term goals. Make sure that you reward yourself as you complete your goals.

Tip If you cannot measure it, you won't know if you have achieved it.

ACTIVITY 10.1 *SMART Goal Activity*

Using the information you have acquired about yourself regarding your vision for your future, establish one long-term goal that relates to your vision statement. Make your goal adhere to the SMART criteria. Once you have written your goal, share it with one other person and tell that person how it meets each SMART criterion.

Now, identify a short-term goal that connects to your long-term goal. Make sure that this goal also adheres to the SMART criteria.

Planning

Your short-term goals provide an action plan for you to achieve your long-term goals. The plans you develop to achieve your goals should identify specific actions that lead to your desired outcomes and the timeframe for completing them. So, once you define your short-term goal using the SMART approach, develop a list of actions that lead to achieving your short-term goal. Identify the information you must acquire, the skills you must use, and the behaviors you must demonstrate to achieve your short-term goal. As you develop plans to achieve your short-term goals, you need to prioritize your key action steps. As you accomplish your short-term goals, make sure to use the information you acquired to inform your subsequent short-term goals and the plans you develop for each of these.

ACTIVITY 10.2 *Planning Activity*

To apply the information from this chapter, complete each of the following steps for yourself. Before you do, review each of the steps described in this chapter.

Career vision statement:

Long-term career goal:

Short-term goal:

Key action steps:

Timeframe:

Outcome:

Current status:

Cautions for Goal Setting and Planning

Too often, people aimlessly worship the goal-setting practice without considering a bigger picture or their surroundings. At one point in your life you might have engaged in a goal-setting exercise just for the sake of setting goals, because others seem to have goals, because the new year has come and you wanted to be a better person, or because your teacher or instructor gave you the exercise. You may be motivated to accomplish such a goal, and, indeed, you can achieve it as long as you plan carefully and take action. There is, however, a danger around many goal-setting practices even if the goals met the SMART principles.

First, highly valuing others' expectations can make you continuously wander, even if you set and achieve SMART goals, without long-term joy and fulfillment. For example, in many cultures, entering a prestigious university is highly valued. In East Asian countries, in particular, parents and students alike allocate the highest portion of their time and resources for college entrance and college entrance exams. In those cultures, entering a highly ranked university is more valued socially than what the student is intrinsically motivated to pursue. Students follow the typical social expectation and set goals accordingly. Because smart kids excel in studying and testing with their perseverance, they achieve their goals—entering a prestigious university. Too often, their life becomes hopeless once they enter college as there is no other goal to pursue. They learn to pursue a socially desirable goal after a wandering period, which does not end in their careers.

Second, if you are too attached to a certain goal, you may lose a holistic sense of your life and life circumstance, including people and opportunities around you. This is called tunnel vision. Even if you are a person who highly values human dignity or the well-being of people around you, your relationship may suffer if you have tunnel vision. Your friends and loved ones may feel ignored or underappreciated. This issue could be avoided or lessened by considering your goals in terms of the multiple life roles that you play before and while setting and implementing goals. Having goals solely in one life domain (e.g., as a worker or a professional) is unbalanced, limiting opportunity for overall well-being of yourself and significant others.

Finally, some people are not goal oriented, and others pursue too many goals at the same time. If you do not have the habit of setting and implementing goals, you may want to start with one goal that you can achieve. If you are, however, a person who sets too many goals at the same time, you may want to consider whether your practice is healthy.

Achievement-oriented people tend to set too many goals at the same time, making their life too busy without a significant return. One solution is to carefully assess the interconnectedness among multiple goals and strategize in a way for you to consolidate diverse activities into one and achieve goals in multiple areas. For example, if you are a student pursuing a master's degree in management consulting with a desire to establish yourself in a related professional association, you can take an internship course to practice consulting skills by volunteering to assist the organization's change process. In doing so, you would meet a course requirement, gain and practice consulting skills, network with already established consultants, and gain a service record in the field. Carefully chosen, one action could satisfy multiple goals, giving each goal full attention. Another example is that if you are a father and wanted to play with your child(ren) and have the goal of losing weight, you could engage in sports activities together.

ACTIVITY 10.3 *Valuable Goals Checklist*

In the table, first list goals that you are considering in the life domains presented. Optionally, you may add a life domain that you highly value if it is not already represented in the table. Second, rate to what extent each of the goals is truly yours using the following response options: *1 = This seems to be someone else's goal; 3 = I am not sure whether this is truly mine; 5 = I have a strong inner desire to pursue this.*

LIFE DOMAINS	GOALS		RATING
Family	1. _____		① ② ③ ④ ⑤
	2. _____		① ② ③ ④ ⑤
	3. _____		① ② ③ ④ ⑤
Career	1. _____		① ② ③ ④ ⑤
	2. _____		① ② ③ ④ ⑤
	3. _____		① ② ③ ④ ⑤

LIFE DOMAINS	GOALS	RATING
Community and service	1. _____	① ② ③ ④ ⑤
	2. _____	① ② ③ ④ ⑤
	3. _____	① ② ③ ④ ⑤
Learning and self-development	1. _____	① ② ③ ④ ⑤
	2. _____	① ② ③ ④ ⑤
	3. _____	① ② ③ ④ ⑤
Leisure	1. _____	① ② ③ ④ ⑤
	2. _____	① ② ③ ④ ⑤
	3. _____	① ② ③ ④ ⑤
( )	1. _____	① ② ③ ④ ⑤
	2. _____	① ② ③ ④ ⑤
	3. _____	① ② ③ ④ ⑤

After completing the table, review whether different life domains are represented by your goals. If your goals are too focused in one area or two, you may want to consider thinking about creating worthy goals to pursue in other life domains. If you have many goals listed, carefully review them and see if you can pursue multiple goals with one project. If you found some goals you can pursue at the same time with one project, draw a line between them. Finally, review your ratings for each of the goals; if you have goals with 1, 2, or 3 ratings, you may want to engage in self-reflection, self-clarity, and visioning exercises. If you have goals with 5's, congratulations. It is likely that the process of achieving them will be joyful and meaningful.

Setting Adaptable Goals and Plans

According to Heraclitus, "Change is the constant in life." Even if you are motivated toward certain goals and make sure that they are aligned with priorities considering your life roles from a holistic perspective, things change. For example, you or a family member may get sick, which will get in the way of executing a plan with the time frame that was set. You may end up delaying the completion of the project or giving it up. Of course, you will be disappointed, and people involved in the project will be disappointed. It sometimes can involve significant consequences if the goal is high stakes (e.g., You may lose a job due to an incomplete project). However, that should not be the end of the world; there are always ways to live a fulfilling life even if you do not get to achieve a few specific goals.

In those circumstances, it is important for you to go back and review your goals and plans. In doing so, consider three potential modifications. First, consider whether the goal could be achieved at a later time. Second, consider whether there are any other activities that will allow you to achieve what you intended. Third, consider whether you should be the person to achieve the goal. If the answer is not necessarily, you may find someone else who can perform the work on your behalf or instead of you. By brainstorming a variety of scenarios, your priorities—what you value most—will become clear. If you build the habit of identifying multiple ways to achieve the same goal even at the goal-setting stage, your adaptation to change will be less stressful; take it as a natural process without perceiving change as hindrance to your well-being and fulfillment.

Implementing and Adapting: Warming Up for Section IV

As you implement your plans to achieve your short-term and long-term goals, you need to monitor and evaluate your plans, relative to your goals. Pay attention to the new information you acquire as you take action. Use the new information that you learn about yourself and your goals to continually inform your planning steps. If the information you acquire seems to reinforce the plans you are implementing, then that information provides you with valuable feedback that you are on the correct course to achieve your goals. If the information you acquire seems to indicate that you need to adjust your plans or your goals, then it is time to return to the self-reflection and self-clarity steps.

As you implement your plans and take actions toward achieving your goals, reflect on what you are learning about yourself and your goals. What do you know now that you did not know when you first implemented your plans to achieve your goals? What does this new knowledge suggest relative to whether you should revise either your plans or your goals? Be careful not to judge any needed revision negatively. It is, in fact, just the opposite. Using new information appropriately is very wise. If you consider the fact that you are always acquiring new information about yourself and your situation, then it would be silly not to take full advantage of this new information as you manage your career. Being personally flexible in this way will help increase the probability that you will achieve a goal that you find desirable and fulfilling.

Summary

People desire work experiences that they find meaningful and enjoyable. Although these experiences are not likely to describe anyone's total work experience, they are essential for satisfying work activity. By focusing on the tasks that are important to you and the skills you enjoy using, you can identify the activities that are most likely to result in optimal career flow experiences for you.

Jihan seems to have developed a vision and goals that highly matter to him. It is likely that he will enjoy a series of fulfilling moments in the future. Looking at his goals, some could be more aligned with the SMART principle, but that will require him to explore his options further. Remaining open to adjusting the specifics of the goals and finding additional elements to pursue is critical. When you are starting out, all goals do not necessarily need to be SMART as long as they are meaningful to you. Having an aim, however, to turn them into SMART goals in the near future can be helpful. For example, Jihan will decide on the specific license shortly and work toward achieving it in a specific time frame. Then, he may decide on whether more qualifications are necessary, what other qualifications are needed, and so on. One minor suggestion to him is to consider different life domains as he seems to be exclusively focused on his career. As he starts a family later on and gains more responsibilities in different life spaces, he will be able to more fully enjoy his life as he pursues goals in a balanced manner.

Identifying long-term and short-term goals as well as plans to achieve your goals are essential steps. Although these steps are grounded in the information that you have gathered about yourself and your potential options, there is always a bit of a gap between the information you have before you take action and the information you acquire as you take steps toward achieving your goals. The new information you acquire as you move toward your goals can be used to inform you as to whether the action steps you are taking are directing you toward the destination you truly desire. Adjust your goals or plans as necessary. New information you acquire will require you to repeat these steps many times in your career as you move toward destinations you desire.

Questions for Reflection and Discussion

1. Review Jihan's story. How did he incorporate his experiences as a child into his current goals? How might you do the same? Try to identify what mattered most to you when you were young. How might that be important to you in your future?

2. Read an autobiography of someone whom you admire. Guess whether this person experienced career success frequently in their work. If you think they did, what did the person do to achieve that success? What can you learn about careers from your subject's experiences?

3. Identify one time when you had to revise your goals. How did you decide to revise them? What information helped you decide that it was time to revise them?

4. What do you think are the most important things to consider in goal setting?

5. How would you assess whether a goal is good or poorly formed?

Additional Resources

The following websites provide more information about SMART goals:

http://www.mindtools.com/pages/article/newHTE_87.htm

http://ezinearticles.com/?Five-Basics-of-the-Goal-Setting-Theory&id=2469149

11

CONNECTING TO THE WORLD OF WORK: RESEARCH, JOB LEADS, AND TREND SPOTTING

OBJECTIVES

This chapter focuses on the important topic of world-of-work information and how to use this information in your career planning. After reading and completing activities in this chapter, you will be able to do the following:

- Conduct occupational research to discover background and emerging trends

- Use observations and people within your network as sources of career information

- Conduct culture audits

- Engage in job shadowing or work experiences to find out more about specific careers

- Find a career focus through integrating self-assessment results and workplace information

- Clearly communicate your career goals using "elevator statements"

- Identify sources of specific job leads, including those in the "hidden" job market

- Continue to spot trends that will impact your career

CASE EXAMPLE

Kim and Kelly had developed a thriving event catering business over the past 10 years, employing eight additional people. They enjoyed their typical break for a couple of months after Christmas and were still traveling in Australia when the world started to shut down due to the COVID-19 pandemic. Friends reached out to them through email and social media when the Canadian Prime Minister said that it was time for all Canadians to come home. By the time they were able to organize flights, they arrived to a country very different than the one they had left. They faced two weeks of quarantine at home before they could even consider what options they might have to continue their business.

Kim is a chef; Kelly managed the catering business and is great at logistics and sourcing innovative products. It soon became apparent, though, that all the large events that they'd lined up for the spring and summer had been canceled. Although they were eligible for some of the government relief programs for small businesses, their savings accounts were quickly evaporating, with no indication of when the restrictions on large gatherings would be lifted. Accepting loans, employee wage subsidies, and payment deferrals were only good business strategies if there was an end in sight with the possibility to make enough additional money to repay accumulated debts. It became clear, very quickly, that Kim and Kelly would either need to restructure their business or find other work.

Kim and Kelly strongly prefer not to relocate. Their contacts are local, they are living in a customized house with the kitchen and storage for their catering business located in outbuildings on their small acreage just outside the city limits. When times get better, they hope to be able to revive their business—perhaps with a smaller team.

Although Kim and Kelly have compelling reasons to look for work locally, almost all job seekers have a preferred place to work. This chapter will equip you to identify job possibilities that are a good personal fit and are realistic in your regional economy. You will learn about sources of information for diverse occupations, techniques for gathering firsthand information about various sectors and organizations, and tips for networking effectively to generate specific job leads. All of these pieces are important as you finalize your career planning and prepare to move into the implementation stage of the hope-action approach to career development.

Conduct Occupational Research: Background and Emerging Trends

As you begin to actively search for work, there are many layers of information to consider. The hope-action approach highlights the importance of ongoing self-reflection, self-clarity, visioning, goal setting, and planning. To prepare to move into the implementing and adapting stages of this approach to career development it is essential to gather current information about occupations, organizations, and industries or sectors you are considering to ensure your career goals are viable in the present economy.

For general descriptions of over 1,100 different occupations, visit O*Net (www.onetonline.org/find/). For each occupation that interests you, read a brief description of tasks, relevant tools and technology, knowledge, skills, abilities, work activities, work context, job zone, education, credentials, interests, work styles, work values, wages, employment trends, and job openings, as well as links to information about related occupations. Drilling deeper into the O*Net resources, you can find regionally specific content.

Surfing the internet and browsing through local and national newspapers can provide more current information about workplace realities; corporate websites, annual reports, professional associations, and sector or industry councils often offer very specific, timely, and relevant insights. Use your O*Net research as a good starting place from which to further explore changes in the dynamic world of work. For example, due to the impending retirement of countless baby boomers, skill shortages are anticipated in many organizations and across industry sectors and occupational groups. However, changes in technology, including advancements in artificial intelligence (AI), have shifted the demand for workers in many sectors and specific occupations. Internationally, there's a widely acknowledged mismatch in workforce supply and demand; at the same time that some jobs are going unfilled due to the lack of skilled workers, individuals remain unemployed, lacking the skills/competencies required for the work that needs doing. Also, global shifts in supply and demand impact local labor markets. In 2019, for example, widespread international uncertainty related to trade and foreign policy negotiations between many of the world's major economies had implications at local levels across the world. This was followed immediately, in 2020, by the global COVID-19 pandemic which had devastating local impacts across the globe. In our highly interconnected global economy, just as in chaos theory, small changes in one area can result in much larger changes elsewhere, and such changes are impossible to accurately predict in advance. Therefore, it is essential to access current, credible news sources for local labor market information before finalizing your career goals.

ACTIVITY 11.1 *Occupational Highlights and Current Trends*

To practice, select two occupational titles to explore. Use the table to anchor key points from the O*Net database. Then, for each occupation, access at least three current sources of information (i.e., information published within the past 3 months). Note any information that confirms or contradicts your O*Net results.

OCCUPATION	O*NET HIGHLIGHTS	RECENT UPDATES (INDICATE SOURCE AND DATE PUBLISHED)

Use Observations and Networks as Sources of Career Information

Once you have gathered and critiqued as much information as possible using print and internet resources, it is important to confirm your findings with people who are actively engaged in the field or organization you are investigating. This is commonly known as *informational interviewing*. (For tips on the kinds of questions to ask during an informational interview, go to http://www.quintcareers.com/information_interview.html.)

Your *network* is in simplest terms the group of people you interact with; it may include family, friends, other students, coworkers at your part-time job, teammates on your soccer team, or friends of friends. As you begin gathering career information (and later, specific job leads), it may be helpful to begin to organize the contact information of these important people into your contacts list.

You may already have people in your personal or professional network who are well positioned to provide you with up-to-date, relevant information. If not, approach people in your network to see if they may know someone who knows someone who can answer your questions. Warm calls are generally easier to make than cold calls; therefore, beginning with people you know and then using their names to open doors with the next level of contacts can make your research process go much more smoothly. Don't overlook the power of social networking through online groups; Facebook, LinkedIn, and similar sites can quickly expand your network and introduce you to relevant contacts in the industry, occupations, or geographic regions that interest you.

ACTIVITY 11.2 *Informational Interviewing*

To practice informational interviewing, begin by asking at least three of your contacts about the two occupations you researched in the previous activity. In the table provided, write down any relevant new information you gather. For example, Kim reached out to the local Chamber of Commerce, the hospital, and the manager of a local hotel to see if they knew of any immediate openings for chefs. Despite restaurants being closed to the public and hotels being impacted by nonessential travel restrictions, Kim learned that several restaurants were staying open for take-out and delivery and that healthcare facilities, especially long-term care homes, were struggling to get skilled temporary staff to cover for regular employees who needed to self-isolate after being exposed to COVID-19.

Sample: Kim's Informational Interviewing Table

OCCUPATION	PEOPLE CONTACTED AND WHEN	CURRENT INFORMATION
Chef	Chamber of Commerce (03/21)	List of restaurants—takeaway and delivery
	Hospital (03/22)	Referral to two long-term care facilities hiring
	Hotel manager (03/22)	Mentioned a cousin's facility with chef away sick

Now it's your turn; complete the following table.

Informational Interviewing

OCCUPATION	PEOPLE CONTACTED AND WHEN	CURRENT INFORMATION

Conduct Culture Audits

Aside from the objective and factual information you access through print and internet sources and personal contacts, there is a subjective side to job search. You are looking for an organization that "fits." Similarly, hiring managers are looking for employees who fit in their organizational culture.

Tip The culture of an organization is like its personality; essentially, it's the blueprint for how things get done.

Values, beliefs, attitudes, and behaviors all contribute to organizational culture. Culture impacts interactions between customers, employees, and management as well as the kinds of results that are rewarded in the organization.

Conduct *culture audits* to identify some of the subtle indicators of what it will be like to work in industries and organizations you are seriously considering. Identify aspects of organizational culture that are relevant to you; this informs your self-clarity in the hope-action approach. Clues may include visible artifacts (e.g., the location and type of building, how people dress, whether workers look happy, indications of on-site daycare or fitness facilities, public signage or sponsorships, recruitment packages that describe benefits or support for education). Also, listen for conversational clues such as whether employees and managers interact with respect, evidence of positioning in the industry, and a sense of hope and engagement or being stuck.

ACTIVITY 11.3 *Culture Audit*

To conduct a culture audit, first identify the specific types of information you hope to collect (e.g., how women are treated in the industry; whether the organization is "family friendly"; how long it generally takes for people to get promoted; the recent impacts of technology; whether most employees stay with the organization for more than 2 years). Next, identify the best source for each type of information; for example, does the organization's website provide any clues? Is there public access to observing the workplace, as in the front end of a community agency or public utility company? Do workers tend to leave the building at specific times of day and line up for public transit? Do they eat in local restaurants? Select one organization to audit. Use the table provided to record your findings. During the physical distancing phase of the pandemic, Kim realized that random visits to any of the places that being considered wasn't possible. However, using webpages, news articles, social media, and phone calls with personal and professional contacts to learn more about the cultures of specific businesses and institutions. Of special interest to Kim was how much autonomy and creativity a chef would with each of them.

Sample: Kim's Culture Audit

TYPE OF INFORMATION	POTENTIAL SOURCE	CULTURAL FINDINGS
How much autonomy and room for creativity would I have here as a chef?	Neighbor who works there; colleague who is a chef in a similar role in a different city	Care facility—prides itself on a standard menu across 25 locations nationally; no variations permitted

Under normal (non-isolating) circumstances, you can likely collect most of your information through passive observation rather than direct contact. However, you may find it helpful to access a "cultural informant." Similar to an informational interview, this informant can help you to understand how the industry or organization operates. Use your network to identify a cultural informant, just as you did for other informational interviews. Questions for a cultural informant may include the following:

• What's great about working here? What's not?

• Who fits in? Who doesn't? Why not? What happens when people don't fit?

• What kinds of things are taken really seriously here? Why?

Now it's your turn; complete the following table.

Culture Audit

TYPE OF INFORMATION	POTENTIAL SOURCE	CULTURAL FINDINGS

TYPE OF INFORMATION	POTENTIAL SOURCE	CULTURAL FINDINGS

Engage in Job Shadowing or Work Experiences

For the next level of information gathering, it may be helpful to arrange an in-person observation. As discussed in the previous section about culture audits, it's possible to observe some workplaces without making any special arrangements.

At this point, your career goals likely aren't completely random. Therefore, now is a good time to arrange to "job shadow" someone in an occupation or specific organization that interests you. If you have access to a job-shadowing or work-experience program within a job search program or at school, take advantage of it.

If you don't have access to a formal program, use your network to identify someone to shadow. Some organizations will have security concerns (i.e., individuals may need security clearance before being permitted onsite) and, clearly, in the aftermath of the pandemic while physical distancing is mandated, random strangers will not be welcome to stand around unnecessarily to watch others work. Where

Tip Even in times of physical distancing, people are moving about to access essential services and many individuals are still working. Whenever you are shopping, using public transit, or accessing a service in your own community, take the opportunity to watch others work. Notice both attitudes and actions (Do the workers seem happy? Engaged? Frustrated? Bored?). Consider what appeals to you about the jobs you observe every day. What doesn't? Why?

Tip Job shadowing provides a unique opportunity for an insider's look at an occupation.

security concerns are the problem, getting a police check and signing a confidentiality agreement may be all it takes to get permission to shadow. In other cases, there may be opportunities to observe from a distance (e.g., Kim could order food to pick up at a restaurant he is considering and, when there, strategically observe the energy of the people he meets with and note the safety precautions that appear to be in place). Job shadowing can be well worth the effort; it provides a unique opportunity to see the day-to-day operations of an occupation, industry, or organization you are seriously considering.

Work experiences, whether volunteer, program related (e.g., practicum, co-op placements, internships, or apprenticeships), or part-time or seasonal employment can also be useful ways to research career possibilities. Similar to job shadowing, work experiences provide an insider's look at a variety of occupations in an organization and industry. However, work experiences go far beyond job shadowing, as you get the opportunity to contribute your skills, develop new ones, build professional relationships, and check out "fit." Take advantage of any work experience opportunities available; they will all help to inform your specific career goals and plans. Kim, for example, thought it might be a good experience to accept a temporary, 1-week contract to fill in for a chef on leave from one of the care facilities, just to get the experience of working in that kind of setting. Although most program-related work experience placements are unpaid, in this case Kim would be paid as a temporary worker.

To fully benefit from job shadowing or work experiences, prepare in advance. Identify specific questions or learning goals. While on site, look for opportunities to demonstrate your knowledge and skills. Where appropriate, offer immediate assistance or do some quick research to help solve problems you observe. Finally, strengthen professional relationships by following up after your job-shadowing or work-experience opportunity.

Find a Career Focus: Integrate Self-Assessment Results and Workplace Information

The hope-action approach begins with self-reflection, self-clarity, and goal setting. Through activities in this chapter, you've accumulated valuable information about occupations, industries, and specific organizations that interest you. The next step is a crucial one, as you integrate all of this information to find a viable career focus (i.e., work you'd like to do and that needs doing).

ACTIVITY 11.4 *Career Options*

Use the table to systematically compare the specific career options you are considering to highlights from your self-assessments and career research. Kim, for example, is focused on finding a management position as close to their small rural community as possible.

Sample: Kim's Career Options

OCCUPATION	SELF-ASSESSMENTS	CAREER RESEARCH	NOTES/NEXT STEPS
Chef	Theme: Creative; values autonomy	During the pandemic, hotels and larger restaurants have laid off workers; restaurants equipped for pick-up and delivery are doing okay. High demand now in care facilities but no room for creativity in those with multiple locations.	Accept 1-week contract in a care facility to confirm insights that this likely isn't a good fit. Approach restaurant owner friend to consider a partnership—offering items from catering menu for pick-up and delivery.

Now it's your turn; complete the following table.

OCCUPATION	SELF-ASSESSMENTS	CAREER RESEARCH	NOTES/NEXT STEPS

OCCUPATION	SELF-ASSESSMENTS	CAREER RESEARCH	NOTES/NEXT STEPS

As you reflect on your findings, keep in mind that your career goals will continue to evolve for the rest of your life. At this stage, you are simply looking for sufficient focus to generate specific job leads. Eventually, you will outgrow any job that may suit you perfectly right now. In some cases, you can enrich your career within the same occupation, sector, or organization. However, in other cases, you'll need to reposition your career to reestablish an optimal career flow. As your personal career journey continues, ongoing self-reflection will lead to enhanced self-clarity, new visions, and adjusted goals and plans. As a result, you'll adapt to personal and contextual changes and strategically implement new career strategies. The hope-action career cycle is continuous.

The next sections of this chapter will equip you to implement the goals you are currently focused on. A helpful first step will be to develop a short statement that clearly communicates your career goal. These are commonly called *elevator statements or 30-second commercials.*

Communicate Career Goals Using Elevator Statements

It is important to be able to clearly communicate your career goals so that others in your network understand exactly what you are looking for and will be able to help you generate work opportunities. Elevator statements derive their name from those brief chance encounters that may open future doors; consider Kim, for example, in a grocery store line behind the owner of a local restaurant that has temporarily shut down in the pandemic. What could open up a conversation to indicate knowledge about the organization and to explore interest in partnering? How could 30 seconds be wisely invested to generate interest in a follow-up Zoom meeting?

As with Kim's grocery store line example, important chance encounters happen anywhere, not just in elevators. Consider the countless people you run into in your typical day-to-day activities (e.g., getting a coffee between classes, at a friend's house for dinner, at the grocery store, or while getting a haircut). Although such encounters are less likely during the self-isolation phase of a pandemic, they still occasionally occur. We've previously discussed the importance of happenstance or serendipity. Your elevator statement equips you to capitalize on happenstance; don't let great opportunities slip away because you didn't know what to say.

ACTIVITY 11.5 *Elevator Statement*

Use the space provided to craft an elevator statement. Be sure it contains two types of information: (a) your career goal(s) or specific job focus and (b) how your qualifications support that goal. Create several statements if you are still exploring more than one career option. Be creative; make sure your elevator statement is memorable and compelling. Kim's statement, to be used with local restaurants, is, "Hi, I'm Kim Campbell—co-owner of Cascade Catering. We've been in business locally for the past 8 years, but as you can imagine, in the current pandemic, all our upcoming events have been canceled. I'm looking for partnership opportunities that will be mutually beneficial—perhaps partnering with a restaurant for pick-up and delivery of items from our catering menu that would be healthy, family-friendly options for quick meals at home. I'm confident that I could bring new customers to your restaurant—over 8 years, we have served thousands of local people at weddings, business events, and fundraising dinners."

Elevator Statement

My goal:

My qualifications:

Identify Sources of Specific Job Leads

You are now nearing the implementation stage of career flow; with plans in place, you are ready to generate specific job leads. You're likely already aware of good sources for advertised jobs (e.g., career services at your college, online job boards [See the appendix at the end of this chapter for links to a selection of online job boards], newspapers, career pages on organizations' websites, and so on). Professional associations and unions may also provide job leads. Many employers use generic resources such as Craigslist to advertise jobs as well as their products and services. It's important to check all of these sources for jobs that might interest you and fit with your qualifications.

ACTIVITY 11.6 *Exploring Advertised Jobs*

Use the table to list 5–10 sources of advertised jobs in the industries you are exploring.

#	ADVERTISED JOBS IN THE INDUSTRY
1	
2	
3	
4	
5	

#	ADVERTISED JOBS IN THE INDUSTRY
6	
7	
8	
9	
10	

You may not realize that the vast majority of jobs are never advertised; estimates range as high as 90–95%, depending on the industry and local economy. To access these hidden jobs, your network will be invaluable; that's one of the reasons your elevator statement is so important. People who know you need to know exactly what you're looking for and how you are qualified for that kind of work; otherwise, they won't recognize the perfect opportunity for you when they hear about it.

Generally, unadvertised jobs cluster into three categories. In some cases, a job is specifically created to suit you because you have made a great impression on a potential employer. This often happens following practicum or work experience placements; after employers have invested several weeks or months in training, they usually don't want to lose a good employee. If at all possible, many will cobble together a job to keep you on the team. Sometimes informational interviews result in unsolicited job offers; these types of jobs also fit in this category.

The second type of unadvertised job is when there is a clear need but nobody has taken the time to advertise it, perhaps because there is no time or human resource capacity to engage in a sophisticated hiring process. In such cases, managers may ask friends, colleagues, employees, or customers for referrals. This is where members of your network can be particularly helpful, sharing relevant leads they hear about. Ask them to tell you about upcoming parental leaves, sabbaticals, or openings due to employees leaving for school, retirement, or other opportunities. Also, ask them to monitor extended health leaves, new projects, or seasonal surges in business.

The third type of an unadvertised job is an internal posting. In such cases, the job has technically been advertised, but only to a select group of people. However, if someone shares such a posting with you, don't hesitate to apply. In many organizations, especially governments and those with unions, it is important to ensure that no one internal is qualified or interested. However, once that has been confirmed, the next step is generally to open the search to external candidates. If you learned of the job before it was publicly posted, your application may result in a hiring decision before others even knew the job was available.

ACTIVITY 11.7 *Unadvertised Jobs*

Use the table to identify 10 potential sources of unadvertised jobs in the industry or sector that interests you.

#	UNADVERTISED JOBS IN AN INTERESTING INDUSTRY OR SECTOR
1	
2	
3	
4	
5	
6	
7	
8	

#	UNADVERTISED JOBS IN AN INTERESTING INDUSTRY OR SECTOR
9	
10	

There are many effective strategies for generating specific job leads. Stay actively connected to the world of work through the following:

- Networking events, volunteer experiences, and work placements

- Warm and, if necessary, cold calls where you actively express your interest in a specific occupation, sector, or industry

- Continuing to monitor publicly advertised openings

Spot Trends That Will Impact Your Career

Your career research needs to begin long before, and continue long after, you land the job of your dreams. As technology continues to change how we work, global economies become increasingly interconnected, and new occupations appear that didn't exist when you began your job search, it's important to monitor those changes and reflect on how they may impact your career. This fits with the adapting stage of the hope-action approach, where you evaluate information that is constantly changing, respond to it proactively, and reenter the self-reflection stage to begin the cycle once again. Some trends can be observed over a fairly long period of time; others, such as the "stay home" mandate during the COVID-19 pandemic, happen much more quickly and have global impact.

> **ACTIVITY 11.8** *Changes in Technology*
>
> Use the table to consider how changes in technology may impact your career and how you can effectively respond. For example, when Kim realized that some regular suppliers were no longer importing the specialty ingredients turning to the Internet offered new sources. Research also revealed that many chefs had now automated kitchen prep functions that previously required additional employees.

Sample: Kim's Changes in Technology Table

CHANGES IN TECHNOLOGY	IMPACT ON YOUR CAREER	YOUR RESPONSE TO THESE CHANGES
Online shopping	Suppliers no longer carrying full range of ingredients I need	Will need to source items that suppliers no longer import May need to make creative substitutions for ingredients in some recipes

Now it's your turn; complete the following table.

Changes in Technology

CHANGES IN TECHNOLOGY	IMPACT ON YOUR CAREER	YOUR RESPONSE TO THESE CHANGES

Some trends are related to global economies; others are industry, occupation, or organization specific. For example, when one local business shuts down, another related business may offer expanded services to fill the gap.

When new standards are introduced in an industry, some occupational groups will be privileged while other workers lose their jobs. Although artificial intelligence has made some jobs redundant, it has resulted in many new jobs related to design, engineering, programming, training, and marketing emerging products.

ACTIVITY 11.9 *Five Trends*

Revisit your career research. Use the table to list five trends that are presently impacting work in your chosen occupation, sector, or geographic region. Kim's research indicates an increasing demand for interesting, family-friendly meals and pick-up/delivery services such as "Skip the Dishes."

Sample: Kim's Five Trends

#	FIVE TRENDS IMPACTING YOUR WORK
1	Families are having meals picked up from restaurants and delivered to their homes

Now it's your turn; complete the following table.

Five Trends

#	FIVE TRENDS IMPACTING YOUR WORK
1	
2	
3	
4	
5	

The ways people work continue to change as well. As you monitor relevant trends, consider whether most of the work in your sector is project driven or permanent, full time. Are workers typically self-employed, contractors, or employees? Where do people generally work? From home? Local offices? Centralized headquarters? Are any jobs generally outsourced to workers from other countries?

ACTIVITY 11.10 *Logistics of Work*

Use the following table to record your findings about the logistics of work in the occupation, sector, or geographic regions you are exploring. For example, Kim found that chef's positions are generally full time but that the ones that offered the most autonomy and creativity were in smaller, locally owned restaurants or institutions. Repositioning the catering business would require a new focus on meeting the needs of families rather than catering to large events.

CHARACTERISTIC	OCCUPATION: _____
Project versus permanent	
Part time versus full time	
Self-employed, contract, employee	
Location: Home, local, head office, international	

CHARACTERISTIC	OCCUPATION: _____
Other (list characteristics)	
Other (list characteristics)	

Trend spotting can help you to predict types of work that may be potentially more stable. Generally, capitalizing on several trends concurrently will maximize your employment security. For example, in a knowledge economy, with an increasingly diverse workforce and a rapidly aging population, it makes sense that a well-educated, multilingual, culturally competent health services manager would be in high demand. Similarly, in a time when robots and artificial intelligence are replacing many jobs, it makes sense that jobs that require complex interpersonal interactions, empathy, and the ability to recognize and work effectively with human emotions would continue to require human input; not surprisingly, then, mental health counselors are identified in O*Net as having a "bright outlook."

ACTIVITY 11.11 *Impact of Trends on Careers*

Use the table to list three possible future careers you are interested in exploring based on the previous assessments and activities completed in this book. Identify three to five relevant trends impacting each and evaluate the impact of those trends on demand for those specific careers. For example, Kim realizes that, due to a trend toward home delivery of food from local restaurants, it might be possible to partner with a restaurant to add some easier-to-transport menu items that had done well in the catering business.

Sample: Kim's Impact of Trends on Careers Table

CAREER	TRENDS	IMPACT
Caterer	Home delivery of family-friendly meals	Although large events are canceled, which had been the foundation of their business, partnering with local restaurants to reach individual families could keep his business alive

Now it's your turn; complete the following table.

Impact of Trends on Careers

CAREER	TRENDS	IMPACT

Have you considered an international/global career? As the internet provides access to career information from all around the world, it has become increasingly easy to monitor and respond to economic trends in other regions. Even if you choose not to leave home (or, as occurred with the COVID-19 pandemic, international travel has been severely restricted), you are likely to be impacted by the global economy or may work in a multinational organization with colleagues from diverse corners of the world; it is therefore important to understand how the global economy may affect your own career.

ACTIVITY 11.12 *Impact of the Global Economy*

Use the space provided to describe the potential impact of the global economy on the careers you are considering. As Kim reflected on this, it became clear that the supply chain had been disrupted. One solution was to shop online for options that could be home delivered; another was to connect with local growers who could offer more secure access to foods with less negative impact on the environment. Recognizing a potential to expand catering to immigrant groups living in the area. Kim also reached out internationally to source recipes and special ingredients that they would find appealing.

Sample: Kim's Impact of the Global Economy Table

CAREER	GLOBAL TRENDS	POTENTIAL IMPACT
Caterer	Online shopping; immigration bringing new food preferences to the area	Stabilize supply chain through local sourcing and shopping online; expand menu to appeal to individuals from different cultural backgrounds

Now it's your turn; complete the following table.

Impact of the Global Economy

CAREER	GLOBAL TRENDS	POTENTIAL IMPACT

Summary

Kim and Kelly, from the case example at the beginning of this chapter, were at risk of losing their successful catering business when the COVID-19 pandemic resulted in cancelation of all of their upcoming events. As a couple, they decided to focus first on Kim finding work as a chef. Kim explored hospitals, care facilities, and partnering with local restaurants to reposition their catering business to provide family-friendly meals that could be delivered to local homes. As hope is the center of the hope-action approach, it is important that Kim's and Kelly's hope be sustained. To do this, hope will need to interact with each of the other elements of the model.

To begin searching for work, Kim engaged in some self-reflection. Becoming a chef in an institutional settingwith no autonomy and little opportunity to be creative. In examining their personal circumstances, Kim and Kelly acknowledged that Kim was the best positioned in the short term to find work to support them both. Kim's values and preferences suited staying entrepreneurial, if possible. Together, they believed that, despite the shocking changes in the global economy, keeping their catering business alive by temporarily repositioning it was the most viable plan.

Kim's reflections led to some self-clarity. As a couple, they knew where they wanted to live and work, and why (i.e., subjective self-clarity, from Hope-Action Theory). However, Kim also recognized the objective reality that there were limited opportunities for full-time work for a chef in the midst of a global pandemic that had closed restaurants and hotels. Kim knew a full-time role in a long-term care facility wasn't a good choice, but was willing to help out on short-term contracts as needed—recognizing that this not only brought in some much-needed income but was also a good thing to do to help the most vulnerable people in an emergency. Kim's reflections and discussions with Kelly also resulted in life role clarity; they accepted that, in the short term at least, Kim was best positioned to bring in the income they needed and Kelly was best positioned to handle the paper-work related to government grants and payment deferrals that would keep the business viable for when events were rescheduled.

In the following questions for discussion and reflection, you will have an opportunity to apply the rest of the hope-action approach to Kim's and Kelly's situation, helping with visioning through brainstorming future possibilities, then setting some short- and longer-term goals with plans for how to achieve them. Finally, you will grapple with how Kim and Kelly could implement the plans you envision. How will they measure success?

What personal flexibility will they need to draw on to experience career satisfaction and success?

This chapter focused on supplementing your visioning and goal-setting activities through investigating the realities of the workplace you will enter. You have learned how to find background information about occupations, industries, and specific organizations that interest you. Other than accessing print and internet-based information, you have learned about the importance of informational interviewing, culture audits, and experiential activities to explore the current realities of work and workplaces you are considering. Many of the activities in this chapter were designed to help you integrate what you know about yourself—the self-reflection, self-clarity, visioning, and goal-setting aspects of Hope-Action Theory—with information you were able to uncover about current trends in specific careers. You learned how to create elevator statements so that you will be prepared to talk clearly about your career goals and qualifications. You also learned about generating specific job leads, including those in the hidden job market (i.e., unadvertised work opportunities). The chapter ended with a reminder that trend spotting needs to be a lifelong activity as you continue your career journey. As the workplace will continue to evolve, you need to stay alert to changes in regional and global economies that may impact your career. This chapter concludes the visioning, goal-setting, and planning components of Hope-Action Theory; you are now ready to focus on strategies for implementing and adapting your career goals.

Questions for Reflection and Discussion

1. Kim and Kelly, our dual-career case example for this chapter, needed to quickly find income sources when a global pandemic resulted in all their upcoming catering contracts being canceled or postponed. Take a moment to reread the case description (from the beginning of the chapter and the conclusion) and note all important considerations that impact Kim's and Kelly's careers. Brainstorm some career possibilities that Kim and/or Kelly could consider. Be creative—the best solution for Kim or Kelly may not be traditional full-time jobs. Engage in some trend spotting. How have catering and other food services changed in recent years? How has technology impacted food preparation? Food delivery? Identify at least one short- and long-term goal for Kim and/or Kelly, supporting each goal with clear and realistic plans for achieving them. Finally, identify practical steps Kim and/or Kelly can take for connecting with their future employer(s) or business partners. How will personal flexibility help

them achieve career success that is fulfilling, meets their financial needs, and serves their community?

2. Conduct a culture audit of your current organization or a local business. What visible artifacts give you tangible clues about what it might be like to work there? What questions do you have that you can't easily find answers to? Who might be a good cultural informant? How could you contact him or her?

3. Work on your elevator statement with a trusted friend, mentor, or coach. Can you say it in 30 seconds or less? Request concrete feedback; ask if, as an outsider, your listener would understand enough about your job of interest to recognize an opportunity if they stumbled across it. Were they convinced that you were qualified (i.e., would they pass on a good lead?)?

Reference

O*Net. (n.d.). *Summary report.* https://www.onetonline.org/link/summary/11-1021.00

Additional Resources

National Center for O*NET Development. (n.d.). *O*NET online.* http://online.onet-center.org/

> The O*NET website is a prime source for U.S. career information. The O*NET database contains information on hundreds of jobs and is free to all users. Individuals can use this site to search jobs, use career exploration tools, and take self-assessments.

LiveCareer Staff Writer. (n.d.). *Questions to ask at the informational interview.* https://www.livecareer.com/career/advice/interview/information-interview

> Being prepared for an informational interview is just as important as being prepared for a job interview. That's why knowing what questions to ask during an informational interview and preparing them in advance is crucial. This resource provides some basic informational interview questions to ask and provides links to additional resources.

Appendix: Online Sources of Advertised Jobs

America's Job Bank—www.jobbankinfo.org/

- Although America's job bank ended operations in July 2007, you can access specific state job banks online

- Use this link to find your local job bank

America's Job Exchange: www.americasjobexchange.com/

- Post your resume and browse through job postings
- Access career centers and resources

CareerJet: www.careerjet.com/

- Search jobs by industry or location

JobBank USA: www.jobbankusa.com/

- Post your resume, search jobs, and access valuable job seeker resources; obtain educational information in the education center

Monster: www.monster.com/

- Create a profile, post your resume/cover letter, and/or search through job listings
- Access career tools and advice

USA Jobs: http://jobsearch.usajobs.gov/

- Search for jobs and access the information center
- Resume builder available

In Section III we encouraged you to use your self-clarity to create a future vision that will excite and engage you. We also guided you in translating your self-clarity into action steps or plans. Collectively, these steps also serve to strengthen your hope. You are taking control of your life and creating a vision that leads to a future you desire because it reflects what you believe to be true about yourself and the world. Once you have completed those steps, you are ready to take action.

Implementing your goals and plans into action requires knowledge, support, and a little bit of courage. Keep your focus on what you learn about yourself and the world as you implement your goals and plans. More specifically, your attention should be on what you know now about yourself and the world as a result of the steps you have taken; how new information informs your current choice; and what you need to do (if anything) to revise your goals and plans. It is all cyclical. These processes continue throughout your entire life. As you learn how to use Hope-Action Theory, you are learning essential competencies for managing the sometimes overwhelming task of education and career planning. You can have confidence in the fact that the different steps in Hope-Action Theory are based on decades of research regarding how to best develop your plans and translate them into action steps to achieve your goals.

IMPLEMENTING AND ADAPTING

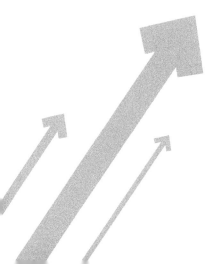

12 MAKING THE MOST OF OPPORTUNITIES

This chapter suggests helpful activities that will enhance your chance to achieve your vision and goals. After reading and completing activities in this chapter, you will be able to do the following:

- Identify educational and professional development opportunities that will help you advance your career

- Create a supportive environment that is surrounded by mentors and like-minded people who share similar career trajectories

- Look for alternative living options to gain financial security and freedom even when you are unemployed

- Seek opportunities that will maximize the development of your competencies that are relevant to your future career options

CASE EXAMPLE

Sara is a 42-year-old mom of two kids in elementary school ages. She returned to work two years ago after about eight years of staying home, but she was laid off recently. Her most recent job was as a cashier at a clothing retail store. She took the position because it allowed her to work in a flexible schedule. Recently, her husband who worked in the hospitality industry was laid off as well due to an economic crisis. She is now desperate to find secure employment opportunities and does not want to go back to part-time positions.

She has an associate degree in customer relationship management. The job she had before giving birth to her first child was a marketing agent in a real estate development industry, which she did for three years. Being in the real estate development industry was her dream in her 20s. At that time, her performance was good, and she enjoyed meeting with potential clients and got excited about their excitement about future possibilities. However, she decided to quit to take care of the newborn baby because she values harmony in the family and wanted to give her kids full attention when they are young.

She has been working with a career coach who helped her envision an ideal future despite her current challenges. She believes that her vision will be the source of energy. Her vision is to develop a motorhome park where millennials can live their lives in an affordable way in a suburban city. She thought that this can be profitable and at the same time meaningful to her and the society. This path is also relevant to her experience as a marketer in the real estate industry. *With the newly crystalized vision, she has been trying to identify opportunities that can help her fulfill the vision.*

Through the visioning and goal-setting activities in previous chapters, you've set clear directions related to your career and life. What opportunities will enable you to achieve your vision and goals? You may be unemployed, employed part time, or employed full time. Or, you may be thinking about retiring soon. Regardless of your situation, we all want to figure out what our next steps will be and how we could get there effectively. This chapter introduces ideas that can help you maximize opportunities surrounding you, including work and personal life.

Pursuing Education and Professional Development

One of the best ways to step up your career is finishing a degree program, if you can afford it. According to the U.S. Bureau of Labor Statistics (2019), the unemployment rate of people with a high school diploma as their highest education was 4.1% compared to ones with a bachelor's degree (2.2%). In terms of median usual weekly earnings, people with a high school diploma earned $730, whereas bachelor's degree holders earned $1,198. To convert it to a year, the salary gap between these two populations is $24,336 a year. If you project it to 10 years or more, the gap becomes enormous.

A cautionary note here is that you will not automatically receive higher income with more security if you pursued a higher-level degree. The benefits of pursuing education vary from one person to another. Because higher education is costly, often involving a student loan, decisions need to be made with extreme care. Otherwise, you will be overwhelmed by debt without being able to focus on work or study. You might not even be able to graduate, ending up wasting time and money.

ACTIVITY 12.1 *Decision-Making for Further Education*

When determining whether pursuing a higher level of education is good for you, the following table can help you make the decision. Some questions can be answered immediately but some questions will require you to explore further and meet people who can provide information. Even after making such an effort, if you are unclear about many of the questions, you probably are not ready to invest your time and money for further education. If you confidently answered them all and feel positive about the potential benefits of further education, congratulations. You probably are ready to put an application together for admission.

DOMAIN	QUESTIONS	YOUR ANSWERS
Career outlook	What career options do I have once I complete the degree?	
	What are the typical jobs that the graduates of the program land?	
	Does my current skill set complement the types of jobs?	
	Are the potential career options something that I will enjoy greatly?	
Finance	How much is the tuition and fees?	
	How will education be funded?	
	If I need to take a student loan, how much will that be?	
	When can I pay it off? What is the rationale?	
	What will be the budget for my monthly living if I started a degree program?	

DOMAIN	QUESTIONS	YOUR ANSWERS
Admission	What are the requirements to enroll in the degree program?	
	Do I have the time, resources, and ability to fulfill them? (Some degree programs require test scores.)	
	Who will be able to serve as my references? (Many degree programs require reference letters.)	
Relationship	What will be the impact of pursuing education on my family financially and emotionally?	
	Is my significant other supportive of pursuing further education?	
	What will be my support system while pursuing education provided that it will require time away from family and work?	
	If I plan to keep my job, is my employer supportive of me pursuing a degree program?	

For many people, pursuing a degree program is not an option to consider. Also, pursuing a degree program is not the answer in many cases. However, pursuing professional development programs can help you be more proficient and position you more credibly. For example, if you work as a coach to help individuals be more productive in their personal and professional lives, it can be helpful to take a coaching training program that will lead you to a reputable certification. For example, taking the Accredited Coach Training Program (ACTP) approved by the International Coach Federation (ICF) will lead you to the Associate Certified Coach (ACC) certification. Pursuing professional development programs can also be costly and time-consuming; therefore, going through Activity 12.1 can be helpful. Typically, professional development programs that lead you to certification are offered by professional organizations or their partners in the profession. They also offer continuing education opportunities to keep you current and confident in your field.

Professional development is not equal to taking a degree or training program. You can start by finding out what competencies are required in your current or future career. With the goal to develop the competencies, you can rely on books, YouTube videos, and professional and personal networks. You might be able to create a challenging project that can allow you to practice the skills that you target.

Joining a Professional Community

Joining a professional community or organization can be extremely helpful as you get to interact with peer professionals. If you work in the field of electrical engineering, you may want to join the Institute of Electrical and Electronics Engineers (IEEE) and attend its conferences. Or, if you work in Human Resources, you may want to join the Society for Human Resource Management (SHRM) and go to a SHRM conference. Your target professional organization will differ depending on your career goal and the field. There are professional organizations that are more practice-oriented and some that are more research-oriented. If you plan to pursue an advanced degree, you may want to explore both worlds. If you've attended a conference before, the next step may be to get involved in committees, interest groups, or societies within the association as a volunteer or a member. You will be able to meet like-minded people who share similar interests as you. Often, they become your mentors and role models. You might meet someone at your career stage, and you could support each other along the way of achieving your vision to work in the field of your choice.

Although you can find information about professional organizations in your field online, you may find a bit more relevant information from your colleagues, professors, alumni, and a seasoned professional who continuously develops his or her skills. You can also reach out to someone via LinkedIn to gather information. You may ask about professional development opportunities along with information about professional organizations. While doing so, you will meet people who are willing to help you and genuinely wish you growth in their professional field, which will work as your support system.

ACTIVITY 12.2 *Three Professional Organizations in My Field*

Gather information from multiple sources to identify three professional organizations in your field and fill out the following information for each of the organizations. Use the information for future planning.

Professional Organization 1

- Name of the professional organization:
- Reasons why you chose this organization:
- Name of the conference:
- Timing of the conference:
- Conference location for the next year:
- Membership fee:
- Conference registration fee:

Professional Organization 2

- Name of the professional organization:
- Reasons why you chose this organization:
- Name of the conference:
- Timing of the conference:
- Conference location for the next year:
- Membership fee:
- Conference registration fee:

Professional Organization 3

- Name of the professional organization:
- Reasons why you chose this organization:
- Name of the conference:
- Timing of the conference:
- Conference location for the next year:
- Membership fee:
- Conference registration fee:

Finding Alternative Living Options

Rent and housing prices are very high in many parts of the world, and sometimes a mortgage takes up more than 50% of the income. It is especially true in big cities such as New York, Washington, D.C., and San Francisco. Many young and mid-to-late career adults look into living in a tiny house for a simple lifestyle that is affordable, autonomous, and environmentally friendly with less carbon footprint. Sometimes, living in a tiny house is transitional when they are financially challenged or need to save a down payment for a bigger house. For example, Jarvis and Jocelyn with two kids are living in a tiny house after paying off $96,000 in debt (Exploring Alternatives, 2018). They are living burden-free, modeling responsible life for their kids. Having felt the burden of being in debt and the liberating feeling of being debt-free, they are saving money for a no mortgage life. According to Jocelyn,

> Living in our house personally, I just feel really free. I feel like we can, because we don't have debt, because we don't have a lot of possessions, and because that truly makes us happy, we have a lot of freedom if one of us decided that we wanted to change our career tomorrow, we absolutely could. If one of us decided we wanted to stay full-time with our kids, we could. We are architecting our life. (Exploring Alternatives, 2018)

Another option for alternative living is a van life.

For example, Eli Peterson, a Youtuber, purchased a $1,500 van and converted it to a camper. He spent his whole college years living in it. With savings that he made, he traveled to many countries overseas, engaging in fun activities such as scuba diving. By pursuing such a passion project, he was able to equip himself with some mechanical skill sets, cooking skills, and a thrifty, yet adventurous lifestyle. Some may say that such a lifestyle will hinder his academic performance as he may sacrifice his time for study and other valuable activities. He graduated in 3 years with a 3.97 GPA for two degrees obtained with academic scholarships, played on a basketball team, and worked as a firefighter in the forest every summer gaining experience and saving money (DIY Eli, 2018).

Both tiny house and van options are not without challenges. If you have a family with school-aged children, it may feel impossible to pursue these options for many reasons. Even if you are a single person or with no children, finding land where you can park a tiny home is challenging. Both lifestyles require a lot of preparation, persistence, and creativity because most municipalities are not ready to embrace this type of alternative living arrangements.

Tiny house and van life may be too extreme for most people. The key message here, however, is to find ways to live and work without the financial burden of following traditional living arrangements and social norms. It may be a good idea to brainstorm ways to downsize the current housing option (e.g., from a single house to a smaller condo) to be ready for emergency and a financially independent lifestyle. If your children became adults and left home, downsizing your house can be an excellent retirement or emergency plan. If you already own a house, you can go even further depending on your local zoning law. For example, a couple living in Seattle built a tiny house as an accessory dwelling unit (ADU) to their house. They live in the tiny house full time while renting out their main house. It became a significant financial source of their retirement. Considering the significant portion that housing cost takes up your budget, knowing about and exploring alternative living options can give you peace of mind for rainy days.

Interacting With Like-Minded People

Interacting with like-minded people can help you explore your interests, develop your skills, expand a network, and create a support system. For example, if you are interested in public speaking, you can join a local Toastmasters club. If you are interested in playing a musical instrument in a band, you may be able to find such a group through multiple ways such as getting to know someone by taking a lesson and finding local musicians online through platforms such as Facebook. Local entities, such as YMCA and Parks and Recreation, routinely organize sports, recreational, leisure, and cultural activities for all ages.

Choosing a group can be intentional, considering your vision and goals. If your vision and goals are set in a balanced manner, your goals may address a variety of domains, such as professional and personal development, well-being, relationship management, and contribution to society. You do not have to tackle all the domains. It comes down to your current needs. If you are in the mode of developing your language skills and cultural understanding of a certain country, you may want to join such a group. If your passion is helping people or animals, you will be able to find local nonprofit organizations with different causes. Through the involvement in the chosen group, you will gain the necessary skills and experiences but also enhances your social network, allowing you to see and connect with role models and like-minded people. Having such a support system, identifying role models, and being surrounded by like-minded people are major factors for you to be hopeful along with having goals (Smith et al., 2014).

If there is no club or organization that suits your interests and goals, you can create one. For example, you can create a meet-up group (www.meetup.com/) or organize an event and invite people. By engaging others in the initiative, you will be able to satisfy others' needs while pursuing your direction.

ACTIVITY 12.3 *Choosing a Social Network*

Explore clubs, groups, and organizations around you for each of the domains in the table. You may fill out the six rows entirely or partially. Keep in mind, however, that fully exploring potential social networks around you will help you achieve your goals. Record the name of the club, group, or organization, what activities they offer, when they meet, and your thoughts about the opportunity.

DOMAIN	SOCIAL NETWORK (CLUB, GROUP, ORGANIZATION, ETC.)	ACTIVITIES AND MEETINGS	THOUGHTS
Career and professional development			
Contribution to society			
Leisure/hobby			

After you have completed the table, examine the list carefully and see which of the opportunities will address your current and future needs, considering your vision and goals. If you do not feel strongly about any of the options, again, you can create one on your own. If that's a possibility for you, describe what the group is about, potential activities, and how you will involve other people.

Ideas for a new group:

_____

_____

_____

Volunteer Work

Volunteering is not just for those who have leisure time. It should not be considered a luxury. You could use it strategically to make your dreams come true. Even if you are too busy studying, working, and/or taking care of the family, you may want to consider volunteering. Why volunteering? Through it, you get to test your interest and competencies in a relatively forgiving environment while contributing to a cause. You can also be exposed to an environment that you may not access if you only pursued a paid work opportunity. Through volunteer work, you may take on a task that requires you to use the knowledge and skills that you are acquiring or aspiring to acquire. If you are studying law, you may volunteer to join a local organization that provides free legal advice. If you plan to become a CPA, you may consider providing free tax-return assistance through a local organization. If you are a member of a club and want to become a leader someday, you may want to volunteer to serve on a leadership team. By doing so, you will get to experience higher-level challenges while getting closer to your dream as you will develop associated skill sets. Employers look for those people who have demonstrated the use of their skills in the real world.

Here are some other examples. Let's suppose that one of your goals is to build something useful by using your hand, but do not have the skills yet. You may take carpentry or machinery lessons or go to a career technical education (CTE) school. An alternative is to join an organization such as Habitat for Humanity where you build houses for those who need them. Along the way, you will learn some basic skills related to your interest area without paying tuition. In your local community, you may have an organization that aims to help others with woodworking (e.g., www.doing-goodwithwood.org/). By being involved in such an activity, you will learn basic and advanced carpentry skills, and as you advance your skills you will also have the opportunity to teach others.

As another example, if you plan to teach or train others in the future, you can start offering free lessons in your subject area. You may reach out to local schools and nonprofit and for-profit organizations and offer such an opportunity. In doing so, you will learn about marketing, develop a lesson plan and teaching materials, and practice teaching skills while contributing to the development of others. This type of experience will help you advance your teaching or training competencies. In addition, your potential employers will be pleased to see these activities in your resume or curriculum vitae, as this is a sign that you are truly interested in and committed to what you aim to do. Endless opportunities exist if you have a will.

ACTIVITY 12.4 *Developing Skills Through a Volunteer Opportunity*

Find out what skills are needed to achieve your vision. You can do so through interviewing someone who already is in your desired state. Or, you may search online using a web system such as O*NET. In the following table, list skills that you want to develop and identify volunteer opportunities that can enable you to develop such skills. End the activity with a reflection and an action plan.

SKILLS TO DEVELOP	VOLUNTEER OPPORTUNITIES

REFLECTION	ACTION PLAN

Exploring Work Opportunities

If you are not employed, while you can engage in non-paid work for your career development, paid work opportunities in the forms of internship, part-time work, and full-time work can be even better if you are ready. Because you are paid, there will be a higher expectation for you to work professionally and deliver quality results. Although the pressure will be high compared to volunteer work, you will get to practice and develop work ethics. If you are employed, you can explore the next work opportunities within and outside of your current employer.

Chapters 13 and 14 address details about how to secure future work opportunities and how to prepare yourself for them. In this chapter, approach work opportunities with a big picture. For example, if your dream is to develop a motorhome park, one option is to study zoning laws in townships nearby and look for lots on sale instead of working as a cashier. However, if there is an opportunity to work part-time in a local campground, that would be a worthwhile investment of your time. Another consideration when choosing a work opportunity is to identify transferrable skills that you can utilize in the future.

ACTIVITY 12.5 *Three Potential Work Opportunities*

In the table, list three potential work opportunities that you wish to have in the next several years. For each option, state the relevance to your vision and experiences, the type of work, and when you can do the work. Practicing this type of exploration will help you make a decision that can facilitate achieving your vision and important goals.

OPTIONS	RELEVANCE TO MY VISION AND EXPERIENCES	TYPE (FULL, PART TIME, INTERNSHIP)	WHEN TO DO
A. _____			
B. _____			
C. _____			

Sara, the case illustration in this chapter, decided to look for job opportunities in real estate franchises by highlighting her marketing experience in the real estate industry. She plans to take required prelicense realtor education upon earning income in order to become a licensed realtor. She does not have to become a realtor to build a motorhome park. However, she thought that she will be able to learn a lot about real estate to navigate through the system. Because it can take more than five years until she can save a down payment, identify a proper lot, and get the development plan approved, she plans to work as an assistant in a realtor's office and then as a realtor. In addition, for a short-term period, she plans to work for a local hardware store to be familiar with different tools and materials that are highly likely to be needed for building a motorhome park site. She signed up as a volunteer for Habitat for Humanity to learn construction skills while helping others.

Summary

This chapter introduced a variety of ways to maximize the opportunities around you, including education and professional development opportunities, joining a professional community, finding alternative living options, interacting with like-minded people, volunteer work, and work opportunities. There can be more types of opportunities than what are introduced. The bottom line is that you can make every step of your action contribute to achieving your vision and goals. When actions are carefully connected to a bigger picture, it is highly likely that you will live a purposeful, fulfilling life.

Questions for Reflection and Discussion

1. Remind yourself of your vision or a long-term goal that you developed through previous chapters. Carefully examine your surroundings including workplace, school, family, community, etc. What are some of the opportunities that can help you to achieve your goals?

2. Let's suppose that you've joined a professional community. What kinds of knowledge and skills do you want to acquire from the community? In addition, what kinds of people do you want to meet and network? Why?

3. If you need to downsize your house within the next three years, what housing option do you plan to pursue? Why?

4. What club, social, or voluntary activities do you plan to pursue? In what ways will they be helpful for your career development?

References

DIY Eli. (2018, February 22). *Life of a college student living in a van + Q&A at the end [Video file]*. https://www.youtube.com/watch?v=VOzQqXhDOls&t=495s

Exploring Alternatives. (2018, January 28). How this frugal family of 4 paid off $96K in debt & built a custom tiny house. https://www.youtube.com/watch?v=GQ6cKZ3Zf9A

Smith, B. A., Mills, L., Amundson, N. E., Niles, S., Yoon, H. J., & In, H. (2014). What helps and hinders the hopefulness of post-secondary students who have experienced significant barriers. *Canadian Journal of Career Development, 13(2)*, 59–74.

U.S. Bureau of Labor Statistics. (2019, September 4). Unemployment rates and earnings by educational attainment. https://www.bls.gov/emp/chart-unemployment-earnings-education.htm

## 13

TURNING POSSIBILITIES INTO REALITIES

This chapter focuses on important job search topics such as resume writing, compiling a career portfolio, and managing references effectively. After reading and completing activities in this chapter, you will be able to do the following:

- Write more effectively

- Customize resumes and cover letters

- Compile a career portfolio

- Manage the impression you create

- Manage references who will confirm your qualifications

CASE EXAMPLE

Jakob has had a fascinating international career in agricultural engineering, living and working on six continents over the past 27 years. He had saved quite a bit from his expatriate salaries and was planning an early retirement—hoping to leave work at the age of 60, in just 3 more years.

Jakob was working on a project in Africa when news stories from home started to warn about international airports and borders closing, nonessential travel being canceled, and countries like Italy imposing lockdowns to try to curtail the spread of the novel corona virus, COVID-19. Although it didn't seem to be changing life much in the community that he was working in, he started to get increasingly panicky calls from family and friends, begging him to come home while there were still flights. As his contract in Africa was winding down anyway, Jakob thought this might be a good time to spend some time at home with his aging parents. He expected all the fuss to die down in a few weeks.

Things changed quite quickly, however. By the time Jakob landed at "home," he learned that he'd have to be quarantined for 14 days—he couldn't even visit his parents or siblings and so was booked into a local hotel. Within days of arriving, some of his riskier investments had lost half their value. With international travel severely restricted for an undetermined amount of time, it seemed unlikely that he'd be able to pick up another international contract right away—and what part of the world would be safe anyway?

Once Jakob's quarantine period was over, he decided to temporarily move into his parents' home for the first time since he'd graduated from university. Since Jakob's parents were within the age group considered to be the most vulnerable, Jakob chose to self-isolate with them until things were back to normal. However, because of the significant losses in his investments, Jakob thought it would be a good idea to try to find some work that he could do from home.

Jakob's international background makes writing a resume challenging as well. He wonders how to adequately portray his diverse experiences, especially in only a couple of pages. Despite being born in the city he was now living in, Jakob had not worked within his country in more than 27 years; he was surprised to discover that local employers devalued anything except local experience.

J akob is a bit worried about his transition from working internationally to locally, especially in the midst of a "stay home" mandate and a global economic crisis. He knows he has much to offer potential employers, especially in international settings. However, he finds the practicalities of communicating those assets quite daunting. Similarly, but perhaps for quite different reasons, you might be a bit concerned about how to clearly communicate your qualifications for the career opportunities that you hope to pursue.

Hope is the center of Hope-Action Theory, and it interacts with each of the essential competencies: self-reflection; self-clarity; visioning, goal setting, and planning; and implementing and adapting. As you work through this chapter, you will need to use each of these hope-action competencies as you begin to implement and adapt your job search plans. Through engaging in practical activities, constructing customized documents, and strategically managing the impression you intend to portray, you will likely experience a renewed hopefulness about securing work that fits you well.

Although your story is likely quite different from Jakob's, we all share the challenge of trying to adequately convey our life experiences in a short resume and cover letter. Increasingly, career experts are also recommending that individuals create career portfolios to showcase their skills. Defining your personal "brand" and managing the impressions others will form of you, both in person and online, are essential to your job search success. Another important asset to support your job search will be excellent references; it's important to coach your references so that they can speak effectively about your relevant strengths. All of these important components of turning career possibilities into realities are discussed in this chapter.

Effective Writing

Your resumes, cover letters, and any other written communication, such as e-mails, thank-you letters, and work samples, all contribute to the impression that your potential employer is forming. Your writing should be professional, error free, clear, and concise. Explain acronyms on first use; although they may be common in a specific occupation or sector, be aware that HR professionals, recruiters, and managers may have different professional backgrounds than you. Your written communication must be generic enough to be understood and interpreted by an outsider but specific enough to ensure that an insider is impressed by your relevant knowledge and competencies. Before sending any written documents, ask a friend or colleague to proofread for you.

Although it may be tempting to engage a professional to write your resumes and cover letters, these documents will generally work better for you if your own "voice" comes through. That doesn't mean that you can't get support from an expert in terms of structure, organization, and proofreading. However, first describe your accomplishments and personal characteristics from your own perspective, interspersing the employer's specific terms where they fit your experience. Only then, after you have anchored what you believe is important to say, consider asking for help in polishing the final drafts.

Use headings, paragraphs, bullets, or other organizational strategies to ensure your information is easy for a reader to understand. Remember that your resume, cover letter, applications, social media and online presence, and related e-mails are all sales tools as well as informative documentation; use adjectives and rich descriptions to make them persuasive. Provide hard data wherever possible (e.g., increased crop production by 25%; negotiated multinational partnership to support food security strategies).

Resumes and Cover Letters

Almost everyone will be asked for a resume at some point in their careers. Whether it's to support a university's co-op office in coordinating work term placements, to leave with a recruiter at a job fair to indicate your interest in a specific company, to justify your request for a raise or promotion in your current organization, or to give to a friend who has heard of some openings at work, it's important to have an up-to-date resume on hand that can be quickly targeted for opportunities that arise. In the following sections, we will introduce two distinct purposes for your resume, four common resume styles, and several resume formats. Although most people would like a resume template to follow, our belief is that the best approach to developing your resume is to customize it for your unique purposes.

Resume Purposes

There are two primary purposes for a resume, and each purpose requires a slightly different format. First, a resume is useful as an ongoing inventory of all your work, education, and relevant life experiences. For this purpose, keep a master resume. Your master resume can be as long as it needs to be; it is never going to leave your computer. The sole purpose of a master resume is to keep track of your work and educational history, including relevant contact information, dates, job titles, courses, memberships, and accomplishments. Do not worry about formatting this version; just keep adding things as you think of them, ideally in reverse chronological order (i.e., most recent first).

The second purpose for a resume is as a sales tool. For this purpose, your resume must be targeted and persuasive. It will be used to convince recruiters or hiring managers that you have what they are looking for, that you are worth considering for an interview.

Tip In essence, the master resume is the unedited history of your life as it relates to your career.

ACTIVITY 13.1 *Creating a Targeted Resume*

To create a targeted resume, follow these simple steps:

1. Open your master resume.

2. Save it with a new file name, specific to the job you are looking for (e.g., your name, company, year, month, date). This ensures that you won't unintentionally submit a resume that was targeted for a different position.

3. Carefully check your contact information and adjust if necessary.

   a. If you are applying to a job that isn't local, consider providing a local address (e.g., a relative's) if possible, to indicate a connection to that region; some employers are reluctant to consider someone from out of the area, worried that there may be travel costs for interviews or relocation. If you don't have a local connection, consider using your cover letter to mention your interest in the region, your plans for relocating, or your willingness to travel to interviews at your own expense.

   b. Make sure your e-mail address is appropriate for professional use. For example, jsmith@x.com sounds more professional than chocoholic@x.com.

   c. If providing your cell phone number, be sure to answer professionally.

   d. If providing a home number, ensure that the voicemail is appropriate and that everyone answering the phone knows that you are applying for work.

   e. Some immigrants and international students use a Westernized name as well as the official name on their transcripts and legal documents. If you choose to do this, make sure that those answering your phone know the other names you are using; also be sure to have some documentation clearly linking both names to you.

4. Apply the "Who cares?" filter to your master resume.

   a. With the job you are applying for in mind, go through your master resume (the one saved with a new name) line by line, asking yourself "Who cares?"

   b. If a line, phrase, or section is irrelevant for the targeted position, modify or delete it (this is why it's essential that you leave your master resume intact and work with the one saved under a new name).

    c. Avoid controversial topics (e.g., hunting) or affiliations (e.g., political or religious) that might unnecessarily and unintentionally have a negative impact on the hiring manager's first impression. However, if the transferable skills from those activities are relevant, consider referring to them in a more generic way (e.g., managed the social media presence for a successful political campaign).

5. Refer to the job ad and all of the research you have gathered about the targeted organization and the specific job. Potential sources include the organization's website, annual report, press releases, or online networking presence (e.g., LinkedIn).

    a. Be sure your targeted resume includes the employer's own words. This is particularly important if there is a chance your resume will be processed electronically, based on a keyword search (e.g., MS Office 365, bookkeeper, customer service).

    b. Match the employer's tone and the organization's brand (e.g., use language and style that is appropriately conservative, creative, or energetic).

    c. Consider creating a profile summary section at the beginning of your resume by highlighting the relevance of your qualifications to the position.

Resume Styles

There are four distinct resume styles: chronological, functional, combination, or curriculum vitae (CV). Choose the one that works best for you each time you create a targeted resume.

A chronological resume organizes your information by date, with the most recent first. Preferred by most employers, this type of resume will work well if you have had relevant education and work experience with a clear progression of responsibility and accomplishments.

A functional resume showcases your relevant skills that may not be clearly attached to relevant work or school experiences. Purely functional resumes tend to worry employers; they wonder what you are trying to hide by not providing dates and specific job titles or education.

A combination resume, just as its name implies, offers the best of both chronological and functional approaches. Generally, relevant skills and personal characteristics are highlighted on the first page of a combination resume, supported by chronological detail about work and school

Tip You only have 20–40 seconds on average to keep a resume reviewer's attention. Your resume must be easy to skim, with the most compelling information near the top of the first page. Use clear headings and bullets to make sure relevant information is quickly accessible. In English, we read top to bottom, left to right. Therefore, the left margin is the second most significant "real estate" on your resume, after the top third of Page 1. Don't clutter that important left margin with dates. Instead, use it for job titles or previous employers. Decide on your structure based on what your targeted employer is likely to be most impressed by; once you select a structure, apply it consistently throughout.

experiences on the second page. This format allows applicants to paint a clear picture of their qualifications (i.e., forming a positive first impression) before the employer has the chance to form a different image based on an apparently unrelated job title or degree. Combination resumes can be particularly effective for career changers and for students who have had a series of summer or part-time jobs that developed relevant transferable skills but, on the surface, don't seem closely related to the targeted job.

Although the term CV is often used interchangeably with resume, within academic and some professional communities, it has a distinctly different meaning. Generally, a CV is longer than a resume and provides reverse chronological lists of relevant professional experiences such as courses taught, conference presentations, theses supervised, publications, and professional service on boards and committees.

Human resource (HR) professionals typically review a lot of resumes. Therefore, surveys about their preferences provide us with important information about how to effectively structure a resume. Over the years, we have drawn from many such surveys and focus groups. Table 13.1 presents highlights about what most HR professionals and hiring managers have indicated they prefer.

TABLE 13.1 Resume Features Preferred by HR Professionals and Hiring Managers

FEATURE	DESCRIPTION
Clear and concise	Relevant information is easy to find
	Resume is one to two pages
Error free	No typing or spelling mistakes
	Use of consistent fonts, spacing, and margins

TABLE 13.1 *Continued*

FEATURE	DESCRIPTION
Targeted	Doesn't seem like it was written for another job
Chronological	Not purely functional (i.e., dates and details are important)
Compelling	Attention grabbing
	Makes a great first impression
Readable	Generally, 12-point fonts that are commonly available on most computers (e.g., Times New Roman or Arial) are recommended (fonts should be no smaller than 10 point)
Action verbs	Each bullet begins with an action (e.g., conducted, developed, coordinated, improved, negotiated)

Resumes come in very different formats and styles. Ensure that you have a clear understanding of the format required for each job you are applying for. Some organizations specify a preferred format; they may want resumes to be submitted on paper, by e-mail (as attachments or embedded in the body of a message), or online (either by attaching a document or by entering information into a standardized form). Using a standardized format makes it easier for the hiring committee to find the exact information they need to inform their decisions. Similar to completing a job application, it is essential to include everything requested and carefully follow the specified format.

Tip Expectations about resume styles and components change across countries. A North American resume is generally no more than two pages, doesn't include a photo, and excludes personal information such as date of birth and marital status. In many other countries, all those items would be expected on a resume.

If submitting your resume on paper, use good quality paper in a neutral color (i.e., crisp white, ivory, or grey). Slightly off-white colors tend to stand out in a stack of plain paper documents. If you have access to a color printer, consider creating a letterhead-style header and using subtle color for headings and subheadings (e.g., dark blue headings with black text). Print your resume single-sided and do not staple the pages (for ease of photocopying by the employer). Your name should be clearly indicated on each page.

If submitting your resume by e-mail, consider phoning ahead to find out how it will be processed. Some organizations block e-mail attachments; it may be necessary to cut and paste your resume into the body of your message. There are compatibility issues between some PC and Mac computers and between older and newer computers. Excessive formatting, especially with the newest versions of a software package, may be unreadable by your recipient. To ensure readability, use a common font such as Times New Roman or Arial that most software packages will recognize and avoid unnecessary graphics or unusual bullets. Consider converting your document into a PDF format; in Microsoft Word, for example, this is an option available when saving files. PDF documents preserve their formats across devices. Keep in mind that many individuals will be previewing their e-mails on mobile devices such as tablets or smart phones. To ensure that your message does not get deleted, the subject line must be clear, and the initial part of the message should be brief enough to convey the key points, convincing the recipient to save your resume for an in-depth look.

In some cases—for example, to cut and paste or upload information into an online form— it will be necessary to convert your resume into a plain text format by using a .txt extension in the document name. In many software programs, this can be accomplished by simply saving the file as a text document; in MS Word, choose File/Save as/Save as type/Plain text). Another option is to open the text editor provided with your computer (e.g., NotePad in Windows; SimpleText in Macintosh), then cut and paste your formatted resume into it.

Before sending an e-mail to a potential employer, try sending it to a friend to see how the formatting looks to the recipient. There may be embedded characters that don't show up on your screen but that fill several lines at the beginning of the document on someone else's. When converting to plain text, it's generally a good idea to remove all bolding, to substitute asterisks for bullets, and to use one consistent font throughout.

For any resume or application that will be processed electronically, appropriate key words are essential. Consider placing a key word summary immediately after your contact information; use nouns and sector or occupation-specific acronyms, provide academic qualifications, and list relevant personal characteristics such as languages. Match your key words as closely as possible to the employer's own language; that is, incorporate specific words from an ad, job description, or information on the corporate website. One caution here is to be sure that you draw on the employer's language without plagiarizing information. You can avoid this by paraphrasing rather than using direct quotes from the employer's brochures and/or websites. Similar to conducting an Internet search using a search engine such as Google, appropriate key words will ensure that your resume surfaces as one that is a close match for the employer's criteria when retrieving resumes from the organization's recruitment database. Because a resume processed electronically loses the traditional advantages of a creative look and a persuasive tone, to be considered at all your message will need to be captured in key words that match the search criteria used. Remember that search engines are literal—they will not "read between the lines" and make assumptions about the transferability of your experiences.

Once your resume is retrieved, it also needs to be appealing to the reader. At this point, all the formatting techniques for paper-based resumes will have impact; ensure a consistent structure, attend to the order that information is presented, use action verbs, and clearly document your accomplishments.

If you choose to post your resume on internet-based job boards, such as Monster and Workopolis, be cautious about privacy and the potential for identity theft. Consider removing identifying information except for your name and creating a new e-mail address specifically for job search purposes. The key, of course, is to remember to check this new address regularly or have messages automatically forwarded to your regular e-mail account.

You may also find it useful to post your resume on your own career-related website. Rather than mixing your career and personal information, it is generally best to keep this separate. If you provide a link to your online resume, a potential employer is quite likely to look elsewhere on your site. This will form part of the first impression you create; therefore, managing your online presence is crucial.

Cover Letters

There are diverse opinions about whether cover letters are necessary or important; some decision makers highly value them while others ignore them altogether. The key is to ensure that your cover letter adds value (i.e., it complements your resume) but that your resume can stand alone if necessary (i.e., there is no essential information available only in your cover letter).

Use the first paragraph of your cover letter to link yourself to the organization (why you are writing). In the second paragraph, describe your interest and fit, explaining how what you have to offer meets their needs and what has impressed you about the organization. The third paragraph provides an opportunity to indicate or acknowledge next steps; in the case of an unsolicited application, mention that you will follow up by phone next week or that you will be in town at the beginning of the month and hope to set up some meetings.

Keep the overall look of your cover letter consistent with your resume—this is part of developing your personal brand. If you created a header with your contact information for your resume, use the same header on your cover letter, forming the impression of a personal letterhead.

Ensure that your cover letters are targeted; it is easy to recognize "form letters," and they rarely add value. Instead, use your letter as an opportunity to let your personality shine through and to showcase your research about the organization you are applying to. Inform the potential employer why you have chosen this particular job or organization: What impresses you about their website? Current projects? Reputation? Use strong, confident language; avoid words like "I hope" or "I feel." If you have relevant quotes from your references—and permission to use them—include some in your cover letter to provide third-party evidence of your claims (e.g., "A recent client wrote ..." or "My marketing professor complimented me on ...").

If possible, address your cover letter to a specific person; check the organization's website or phone the office if necessary. Make sure names are spelled accurately and preferred titles are used (e.g., Dr., Ms.). Many people have clear preferences and may become annoyed with an incorrect salutation; clearly, this wouldn't contribute to a great first impression. Don't make assumptions about gender identity; initials don't provide that information, and many first names (e.g., Kim, Jasjit, Pat) are used by both men and women, and it is increasingly common for individuals to choose their preferred pronouns. If, despite all your best efforts, you can't find an individual's name, address the letter generically—for example, Dear Hiring Committee or Dear Operations Manager—or use a memo format and avoid the "Dear" line entirely.

Career Portfolios

Career portfolios are becoming increasingly popular as a tangible way to document and communicate career accomplishments. Artists, actors, and architects have used portfolios for years; now they are becoming standard for other occupations as well. Many high schools and postsecondary institutions require students to build a career portfolio as a graduation requirement.

Although much attention may be paid to the format of a portfolio—for example, web based, binder, portable file box, or a more artistic representation using scrapbooking techniques—the reality is that most employers will not ask to see your portfolio and, if you present it, won't take the time to look through the whole collection. It makes more sense to use your portfolio as a personal organizing tool, set up in a way that it will be easy for you to find what you need for specific purposes (e.g., a specific sample of work for a job interview, a transcript to support an application to grad school, or contact information for a reference you want to use for a particular opportunity).

Similar to your master resume, if you are building a portfolio for your own personal use, there is no need to worry about an attractive format and no need to limit the number of items you include. Rather, begin to collect any information that may be potentially useful in your future job searches and select a framework or filing system that makes intuitive sense to you; the goal is to ensure that you can find exactly what you need without having to waste time looking for it.

To get you started, here is a list of potential portfolio items. Some may not be relevant for you; others, that may present wonderful evidence of your qualifications, may not be listed here:

- Academic documents (certificates, diplomas, transcripts)

- Agendas or programs, especially those listing you as event organizer or presenter

- Marketing materials (brochures from programs or projects you contributed to)

- Performance reviews or evaluations

- Photographs, if they illustrate an accomplishment supporting your application

- Plaques or group awards (include a photocopy or photo)

- Publications such as newsletter/newspaper stories about you or your projects, brochures

- Recognition from others (awards, references, thank-you letters, or e-mails)

- Resume or professional profile/biography

- Work samples (excerpts of school projects, published articles, photos of projects)

  ○ Be sure you have permission to share work samples, especially if the project was proprietary or contained confidential information. Sometimes you can remove the private contents but still showcase the format of the report you wrote.

Depending on your comfort with computers, your preference may be to organize your portfolio as a computer-based file or as a website. The key is to be intentional about saving evidence of your accomplishments that can support future job applications and career conversations.

Impression Management

Similar to how "branding" contributes to an organization's marketing strategy, defining and consistently using your own personal brand will contribute to your successful job search. Just as organizations re-brand to approach a new target market, so too might your personal brand need to be adjusted as you transition from school to work or between different occupations or sectors. Recent research has also confirmed what we'd long assumed: Hiring managers respond to subtle self-promotion and "ingra-tiation" (i.e., they want to feel appreciated and respected and that they're hiring the best person for the job; Waung et al., 2017).

There are five distinct arenas in which to manage your professional image: on paper, by phone, when video-conferencing, in person, and online. Tips for impression management in each of these areas are presented in the following sections.

Paper

As described in the resume and cover letter section of this chapter, potential employers will form an impression of you through your written communica-tion. They will notice whether it is clear, concise, error free, and interesting. Does your e-mail address convey the image you hope to create? Consider choosing subtle colors, appropriate fonts, and attractive design elements to ensure that your documents stand out from the rest, while portraying a professional look.

Phone

As previously discussed, consider carefully which phone numbers to pro-vide to potential employers. Your voicemail should be clear and professional. Whenever you answer the phone (day, night, or weekend), assume that it could be a call from a potential employer. If using a phone that others may answer (e.g., a home phone or a number shared with roommates or family members), get their commitment to support your professional image by answering the phone appropriately and taking a detailed message.

Video-Conferencing

When video-conferencing, ensure that your camera, microphone, device, and Internet access are high quality and reliable. Also consider lighting, any background that's visible, and how you're dressed and groomed—you may be looking at your photo displayed in a tiny box at the side of your screen, but your viewers may have video displayed on a wall-sized screen in a conference room! Also, especially when working from home, ensure that others are aware that you're in a professional meeting. There are many examples of children stopping by to ask for treats or family members running water or using a noisy blender in the background.

In Person

What is considered appropriate workplace language and attire changes quite dramatically across occupations, sectors, and even levels within an organization. As you develop your personal brand, choose a style that will fit with the specific organizations you are targeting but that is also a good personal fit for you; although it's possible to "be someone else" in a job interview, it's very difficult to be painted into a corner where you can't be yourself long term. As you research occupations and organizations, notice how people dress, interact, and speak. You'll naturally be attracted to some organizations more than others. However, recognize that some of the people you encounter in the workplace have earned the right over time to their unique, perhaps somewhat eccentric, personas. Be constantly aware of the professional image you hope to project; if in doubt, for interviews and the first few days of work (i.e., as you build those important first impressions), err on the conservative side.

Remember, it is not just your clothing that contributes to your personal brand; consider how your hair, scents, shoes, piercings, tattoos, accessories, and general hygiene either support or detract from the impression you hope to create. Similarly, it is important for you to understand workplace etiquette; what is considered acceptable or rude changes subtly across organizations, regions, and cultures. Observe, ask questions, and find a well-respected "cultural informant" who is willing to be honest with you about what is working, what is not, and how to effectively manage the impression you are creating.

Finally, carefully consider the key messages that you want to convey when you meet someone in person—whether at a networking event, job interview, or your first days at work. Adjust your elevator statement or 30-second commercial and don't lose your authenticity; no one wants to think that you're simply reiterating a rehearsed statement. You will have different key messages for different audiences; however, be strategic about the words you use that will contribute to the impression others form of you. Integrating key words, trends, and your knowledge of current workplace realities will convey the message that you fit and have high potential to contribute.

Online

It's also important to consider your online presence. Have you Googled your name lately? Potential employers and recruiters likely have, as they were short-listing interview candidates. Consider the impression they may have formed as they looked at the associations you are linked to, reviewed your Facebook or Instagram, or checked out your personal website or blog. There have been many high-profile examples of how an online presence has worked well (e.g., President Obama's successful campaign) or not (e.g., when another presidential hopeful's young daughter publicly endorsed Obama rather than her own dad as a presidential candidate). There are countless resources to help you manage your online presence; just Google "online impression management job search" to get you started.

ACTIVITY 13.2 *Impression Management: What's Working? What's Not?*

Use the following spaces to record some of the reflections about the impression you hope to form. What's currently working and what's not in each of these arenas? (e.g., Phone: What's working? My voice-mail has a professional greeting. What's not working? Sometimes my roommate does not take detailed messages.)

FORMAT	WHAT'S WORKING?	WHAT'S NOT?
Paper		
Phone		
In person		

FORMAT	WHAT'S WORKING?	WHAT'S NOT?
Online		

Managing References

Your referees will also impact the impression you create; select them wisely. Do some "due diligence" before submitting a referee's contact information—the best referee for one position might be the kiss of death for another if that individual doesn't have a good reputation with the decision makers at your new organization. Don't make assumptions that someone will speak highly of you; if in doubt, ask directly, especially about areas of potential concern (e.g., "What will you say about why I left the organization?" or "How will you answer a question about my weaknesses?"). Some individuals are generally cautious or reserved; they'll never speak highly of anyone—but your potential employer won't know that. Choose referees who will speak honestly, enthusiastically, and positively about your work.

Select referees who have specific and relevant knowledge about you. The CEO of your organization may not actually be able to offer details about your specific career accomplishments; the project manager from one organization may not be able to speak about your competencies as a project manager yourself somewhere else; your best friend's dad, despite his impressive position in the industry, may know nothing about your ability to network computers. Such contacts may be wonderful for opening doors as you research opportunities; professional referees, however, need to be able to speak in a concrete way about your ability to perform the specific job you've applied for.

Do not be afraid to coach your referees. They may need reminders of your specific accomplishments while you worked for them or when you were a student in their classes; there's no reason to expect a past supervisor, instructor, or colleague to recall your past accomplishments in vivid detail without some prompting. If you have been building a career portfolio, it will be useful at this point to help you identify and document accomplishments related to each of your selected references.

Also, inform your referees of professional development and career accomplishments since you left their employ (or since you finished the course you took from them). It can be helpful to give your referees a clearly organized table listing key job requirements in one column and specific details about how you match those requirements in the other (see Table 13.2). Also, provide your referees with the targeted resume submitted for the job you are asking them to endorse you for.

TABLE 13.2 Linking Accomplishments to Job Requirements

JOB REQUIREMENTS	MY QUALIFICATIONS/ ACCOMPLISHMENTS

Be sure to check in with your referees each time you plan to use their names. Confirm that their contact information is current, that they'll be available to respond quickly to requests, and that they are clear about the specific job you are applying for. They might choose different stories or examples, for instance, if they know you are applying for an accounting job with a national grocery retailer versus a hotel chain.

You may occasionally need a reference on very short notice; if your best referee is out of town, it may be helpful to have some written recommendations on hand to share with your potential employer. Also, a good letter of recommendation written soon after a major accomplishment will likely provide richer detail than if a referee is asked to speak about the accomplishment several years later.

Finally, if your referees are from a different time zone or may answer the phone in a different language, make it easy for your potential employer to connect. Provide exact dialing instructions (complete with country code and, ideally, with a direct line or specific extension). Calculate time zones (e.g., "If you phone at 4:00 p.m. here, you will be likely to reach him in the office because it will be 8:00 a.m. there"). And, if necessary, provide key local language phrases written out phonetically that will get the right person on the phone in a foreign country.

Summary

This chapter has focused on the logistics of turning your career possibilities into realities, through creating effective resumes and cover letters, building a career portfolio to document your accomplishments, managing impressions and your personal brand, and selecting and coaching your referees.

Tip Before discarding a potential career portfolio "artifact" (e.g., a performance review, feedback on a complex project, thank-you card from your last day at work), consider snapping a picture of it on your phone and then save these images as part of your portfolio.

Revisiting Jakob's unique situation in our case example introduced at the beginning of the chapter, it's easy to see that all of these tasks will be important considerations for him. As you'll recall, Jakob didn't have any local work experience; however, he did have 27 years of international experience that has resulted in countless relevant transferable skills. Ideally, he has held on to relevant certificates, commendations, and samples of his work, providing evidence of his accomplishments. Realistically, however, he may have saved very little; people who relocate internationally generally purge before each move, and what they do have is likely to be buried in a box in storage.

Therefore, as part of his job search preparation, Jakob may need to strategically gather some work samples and reference letters; he may also find it helpful to take on specific local projects that will result in great references and evidence of his skills. Jakob's referees may be scattered across the globe; he may need to reconnect with them, update them on his current career context, and provide them with a copy of his targeted resume. As Jakob's career experience is international and his network is already global, he may benefit from constructing a professional online presence with a blog, a LinkedIn profile, and a web-based career portfolio and resume. If he chooses to explore international opportunities that he can fulfill by working virtually from home, Jakob will need to clarify resume or CV expectations. If using the resume he'd prepared for his most recent project in Africa, for example, he may need to make significant adjustments to ensure it conforms to local standards. Jakob, like all global careerists and others transitioning between countries or sectors, will need to build his professional "brand" and customized job search tools to support it. In an ideal world, he would have begun his job search 6 months to a year before relocating. However, in the context of sudden changes due to the global pandemic, like people all over the world, Jakob will need to customize his approach quickly to meet immediate emerging needs on projects that he can complete while working from home.

Questions for Reflection and Discussion

1. In what ways are your challenges similar to Jakob's? In what ways are they different?

2. From a hope-action perspective, how will ensuring that you have the right tools in place impact your chances of success as you begin looking for work or prepare to reposition your career?

3. Which of the tools and strategies described in this chapter—resume, cover letter, career portfolio, impression management, references, and so on—will be easiest for you to prepare? Which will be the most challenging? What's the first step you will take to get them in place?

Reference

Waung, M., McAuslan, P., DiMambro, J., & Międoć, N. (2017). Impression management use in resumes and cover letters. *Journal of Business & Psychology*, *32*(6), 727–746. https://doi.org/10.1007/s10869-016-9470-9

Additional Resources

Doyle, A. (2018). Tips for asking for a letter of recommendation. *Balance Careers*. https://www.thebalancecareers.com/tips-for-requesting-letters-of-recommendation-2062964

In this informative article, Doyle addresses who to ask for a reference and how to ask. Links to other resources are also provided, including sample reference letters.

Doyle, A. (2019). *Tips for dressing for job interview success*. Balance Careers. https://www.thebalancecareers.com/tips-for-dressing-for-success-2061336

  Provides tips on interview attire to contribute to effective first impressions, with specific examples of appropriate men's and women's attire.

Government of Manitoba. (2014a). *A guide to building a career portfolio*. http://www.manitobacareerdevelopment.ca/cdi/docs/bldg_portfolio.pdf

  Provides an overview of the career portfolio development process (e.g., collecting, selecting, and organizing portfolio content) and how to use a portfolio for career planning and job search.

Government of Manitoba. (2014b). *A guide to writing cover letters and other employment-related letters*. http://www.manitobacareerdevelopment.ca/cdi/docs/writing_cover_ltrs.pdf

  Includes an overview of several types of employment-related letters including cover letters, thank-you letters, and reference letters.

Government of Manitoba. (2014c). *A guide to writing resumes*. http://www.manitobacareerdevelopment.ca/cdi/docs/writing_resumes.pdf

  Provides an overview of how to craft a targeted, visually appealing resume pulling from what is known about the self and the desired position/organization.

Jacobs, D. L. (2013, February 19). *Five top resume turnoffs*. Forbes. https://www.forbes.com/sites/deborahljacobs/2013/02/19/five-top-resume-turnoffs/#2d03d39eebbe

  Details five common resume mistakes and presents strategies for addressing them.

Koblyk, L. (2019, February 14). *The secret CV: Documenting work experiences that don't seem relevant, but are*. University Affairs. https://www.universityaffairs.ca/career-advice/careers-cafe/the-secret-cv/#new_tab

  Describes a "secret CV," a document containing things that someone is proud of but just hasn't figured out how to best articulate. This can be a helpful document to keep track of accomplishments that may not be relevant for a current position but could be relevant in the future.

Osmundson, E. (2015, January 20). Raising the bar on references. NE Pork. http://www.nepork.org/raising-the-bar-on-references/

  Provides details on how to compile a list of potential references and best practices for requesting, tracking, and using references in job searches.

Shane, J. (2018). Is that me you're referring to? *USA Today Magazine, 146*(2872), 50–51.

  Details several ways a bad reference can impact job search and career success, including sample responses from reference-checking questions.

van den Beld, B. (2014, July 8). *How to see private Instagram photos without an account*. State of Digital. https://www.stateofdigital.com/instagram-privacy/

> Outlines how selecting privacy settings isn't always as straightforward as social media users would hope. Specific strategies and precautions are detailed.

Weiss, T. (2008, March 26). *Entering the workforce: Give your career a flying start*. Forbes. http://www.forbes.com/2008/03/26/workplace-dress-behavior-lead-careers-cx_tw_0327etiquette.html

> Provides practical tips and insights for those important first few weeks at a new job.

ENGAGING THE SEARCH: GENERATING LEADS, NETWORKING, INTERVIEWING, AND MAKING A SUCCESSFUL TRANSITION

## 14

OBJECTIVES

This chapter focuses on the job search and related skills. After reading and completing activities in this chapter, you will be able to do the following:

- Generate work opportunities

- Network effectively

- Master the interview process

- Successfully transition to the next stage of your career

CASE EXAMPLE

Steve really enjoyed his work as a boilermaker and, since completing his education when re-careering over 10 years ago, he has been working almost full time maintaining equipment at remote sites in the oil and gas sector. Even during the economic downturns in that sector, his specialized role in maintenance had been relatively secure. He flew in for 12 days each "shift" and then was home with his wife and young son for over a week at a time in between. However, at least once or twice each year, they'd worried that he'd be in the next set of layoffs. Despite full-time work at a very good salary, his work felt increasingly precarious.

Although he'd avoided all previous layoffs at his site, the health-related impact of the global COVID-19 pandemic resulted in a full closure and the layoff of all nonessential staff. Financially, Steve had saved enough that, with a small severance package, accumulated vacation pay, and employment insurance, he could manage without work for a year or more. His wife was working from home and still earning a full professional salary with benefits that covered the family. Their son's daycare had closed due to the physical distancing and "stay home" mandates, so in some ways it was great for them that Steve could be home full time to fill the childcare gap. However, they both saw this as a short-term solution. Steve decided to also use this time to prepare for a transition out of the oil and gas sector. He was especially interested in the emergence of "green energy" and thought that work in that sector might be a better fit with his personal values as well as his need for a steady income.

Steve's story highlights the complexity of lifelong career management. Even when he had achieved the career of his dreams, the impact of external factors created changes beyond his control. Rather than being derailed by those changes, he took the opportunity to pause, consider all his life roles, reflect on his values and current needs, and make plans for the future. This chapter provides strategies for generating specific work opportunities, mastering the interview process, and navigating challenging transitions to result in a fully satisfying next step on your career journey.

Generating Work Opportunities

This is the culmination of your career planning and work search preparation, building on your self-reflections, goal setting, and comprehensive research. After you've developed basic tools such as resumes, cover letters, and career portfolios, you are ready to respond to specific work opportunities.

This step will be most effective if you have a clear goal in mind—work that is realistic, interesting, and worth actively pursuing. Perhaps counterintuitively, being open to "any job at all" is unlikely to generate specific leads. It's like being open to going to any university: Where would you apply? Or moving into any apartment: Where would you start looking?

So, before moving forward, revisit your goals and action plans. If your goal is a bit fuzzy, review or revise self-assessment activities you've completed. It may be time to face your fears or reestablish supports. In essence, sometimes it is necessary to spend time quietly preparing for the stress and turbulence that tends to accompany transitional times.

Once you have a clear goal in mind, it is time to generate concrete leads. Begin by revisiting your career research and capturing everything relevant to your chosen direction. Visit websites for the organizations that interest you; some may have specific career opportunity sections. Also, Google the occupation, industry, or organization name for recent press releases or news items; although these generally won't list job openings, they can provide important information about emerging trends, funding or policy changes, stock prices, new projects, or changes in leadership. For larger organizations that tend to be in the news daily, narrow your search (e.g., "organization name," "press release," "month year").

Also, subscribe to listservs that share job openings, such as professional associations. Do a current Google search using the occupation, industry, or organization names you have selected and limit the search with your preferred region.

Indeed has quickly become an important place for employers seeking to post jobs and search through resumes and job seekers searching job postings, company profiles, and salaries. Job seekers can start by visiting its website (https://www.indeed.com) and entering a job title, keyword, or company as well as location. Results can be narrowed through a variety of filters (e.g., salary, job type).

Steve's job loss was in the midst of a global pandemic, where it was impossible to be "out and about" generating job leads. However, in more typical times it can be helpful to create a list of relevant career fairs in your area and plan to attend some; Google "career fair" in your region and "month year." Aside from being a source of current openings, career fairs can provide general information about occupations, sectors, or organizations that interest you and be an opportunity to talk to an employee to get an insider's look. Keep in mind that the insights are from a corporate representative's or recruiter's perspective; as his or her role at the career fair is to "sell" careers, you are not getting an unbiased view.

Depending on your specific career goals and the current economy, you might also find it helpful to register with one or more recruiting firms; avoid signing a contract with a recruiter that prevents you from working with other recruiters or accepting a job that you find on your own. Recruiters may have exclusive access to some local employers (i.e., all hiring is done through the recruiter); because they are constantly engaged in hiring, they will also have a good sense of the current trends in your field. Feedback from recruiters about your resume, experience, and overall presentation in terms of industry or organizational fit may be invaluable; be aware, however, that most recruiters have standard resume formats and their requests for changes may be specifically for their own internal use.

Temporary job placement firms may also be an effective way to connect to the workforce. Short-term contracts provide you with an insider's view of an organization (or, perhaps, several organizations). Some employers have a policy of hiring full-time employees only from their temporary workers. Placement firms generally have clear policies about how employers can buy you out of their contract if they want to bring you on board before the original term has ended.

ACTIVITY 14.1 *Contacts and Leads*

Use the table to record specific sources of job leads in the careers that interest you based on the assessments and activities you have completed throughout this workbook. For example, once you identify an organization that interests you, write the organization's website address in the corresponding space.

TYPE OF RESOURCE	SPECIFIC SOURCES
Organization's website	
News and press release	
Listservs	
Job boards	
Career fairs	
Recruiters	
Placement firms	
Other	

Networking Effectively

Your network will be a useful support at all stages of the hope-action approach. In the stages from self-reflection through planning, your networking efforts were focused on gathering background information to inform your career decisions. During the implementing stage, however, your networking will be more targeted as you seek contacts in specific occupations, industries, organizations, professional associations, or geographic regions to access any specific job leads they may know about. Although statistics vary according to industry, region, and economic conditions, it is generally accepted that about 80% of job openings are filled through networking; that is, the openings may not have been advertised and, even if they were, the individual hired was referred by a contact. It is essential to tap into this "hidden" job market if you want to maximize your chances of finding great work.

To begin this new stage of networking, revisit the map of your existing personal and professional network. You may have created one when reflecting on your sources of support (in the **Tip** Your network will be most effective if it is nurtured and not just activated at crucial times.

self-clarity stage) or conducting career research (in the planning stage). If not, use your contact lists—in your e-mail system, mobile phone, Facebook, LinkedIn, Twitter, or Messenger accounts—to begin your data mining.

Activate your network by reconnecting with key contacts, updating them on your progress and career decisions, and asking for their insights about whom to talk to and where to find current work opportunities. If you are in regular contact with your network, they won't be surprised to know you're looking for work. In fact, they may already have mentioned you to key contacts who they know might be hiring. Be sure to keep your network up to date regarding your changing interests and goals, major accomplishments, and job search process.

Psychologist John Krumboltz (2011), in his work on happenstance, said that uncertainty is natural and that plans emerge and evolve. This has never been more true than it was for Steve, job searching in the midst of a global pandemic that had, quite literally, shut most of the world down and sent people home. The key, however, is to remain curious and active; you are far more likely to generate work opportunities at a networking event (or even a sports activity or family dinner) than if you are chained to your computer passively waiting for an employer to notice the resume you posted online. Even in the midst of the "stay home" mandate, it's possible to strategically connect with others by phone, video-conferencing, or social media. Many individuals can identify "lucky breaks" in their careers; however, as Roman philosopher Seneca has been credited for saying, "Luck is what happens when preparation meets opportunity."

To increase the likelihood of lucky breaks, formulate specific requests for your network contacts (e.g., "Do you know anyone working at XYZ company, ideally in green energy?"). Through his research, Steve discovered that boilermakers like him were employed in building and maintaining air pollution abatement systems—that sounded like a great fit between his skills, experience, and desire to become employed in the green economy. Your preliminary conversations will likely take place with people who you connect with casually on a daily basis; although they're unlikely to be in a position to hire you—and may not even have direct contact with your potential employer—their referrals will be warm rather than cold calls.

At this next level of networking, you are much more likely to be moving closer to people who will have direct leads, so be sure to ask for those leads. The good news is that, again, your next calls will be warm rather than cold. Although with those closest to you it's unlikely that you would use an elevator statement (i.e., a short description of what you want and how you're qualified), you may find it helpful to write out some key points to cover with your second- and third-level contacts as these will be people you don't know personally or at least not very well.

Do not wait for a job to be advertised. Make a list of all employers of interest to you and contact them directly to see if they are considering hiring. Ask potential employers if they are available for an informational interview. Even if employers that interest you don't have a suitable job opening, some may have other contacts in their professional networks looking for someone with your skills. Keep in mind the high number of unadvertised jobs and the various formats they may take: parental leaves, relocation, expansion, seasonal hiring, new projects. Many employers have even created new positions simply after meeting an interesting individual and seeing great potential.

During this active stage of work search, under normal (non-"stay home") conditions, it would be important to attend as many networking events as you can fit into your weeks (and, of course, can afford). To effectively network at events, act like a host rather than a guest. Proactively introduce yourself; if you know others at the event, introduce them to each other. Use small talk to find commonalities but focus on engaging in authentic, rich interactions. Be positive and respectful; spend more time listening than talking. Create a professional impression by demonstrating cultural competency, industry knowledge, and a sincere interest in sector-related conversations. If alcohol is served, either avoid it altogether or make one drink last through the whole event. Your goal is to generate leads, sound professional and articulate, and remember subtle details that come up in a myriad of conversations; you need to remain sharp and focused. Aim to leave each conversation with a concrete lead, referral, tip, or new perspective. Sometimes your contacts will think of important information after you leave; be sure to give them your resume or business card with your specific information request on the back or offer to follow up by e-mail if that would be more convenient for them. With more tech-savvy contacts, consider mobile apps (e.g., LinkedIn) that facilitate sharing contact info by simply tapping your phones together (e.g., Fast Share, Airdrop). Ensure your social media profiles are all professional and up to date; your network will expand (or contract) as people find you online and form impressions about your fit with their industry or organization; similarly, you can find out a lot about the people you meet by looking them up online.

Nurture your network; networking that is one sided, that is all about you, gets stale very quickly. Effective networking is not a contest won by collecting the most business cards or having the most populated database. Rather, it is based on mutually rewarding relationships as you exchange information, insights, leads, and supports. Be sure to follow through on leads from your network and update those who have given you leads on your progress. Effective networking will continue to benefit you throughout your career by opening doors, sharing industry updates, providing candid feedback, and, through relevant connections, enhancing your professional image.

Expand your horizons. Engage your network in helping you consider all possibilities. You may be focused on securing full-time work; in an increasingly "gig economy," might two part-time contracts or a short-term project potentially work? Being open to alternatives could unleash countless possibilities; employers who don't have a full-time position in the budget might consider bringing you on board on a part-time or contractual basis.

Are you committed to a specific geographical location? If not, begin your search in a circle close to home and gradually widen it. Take a similar approach with other cities or countries where you have contacts in place (e.g., if you are based in Nebraska but have family in Tennessee, it may make more sense to expand your work search to Tennessee than to Kansas, even though Kansas is geographically closer).

As you learn details about specific work opportunities, revisit your self-assessments to check for a good fit. Does the specific opportunity capitalize on your strengths and skills? Does it interest and intrigue you? Will your key reasons for working, that is, your work values, be satisfied? Does the organizational culture suit your personal style? How will accepting this job impact the significant people in your life? Does it provide opportunities for ongoing career development? Does it fit with your leisure activities and lifestyle priorities?

Mastering the Interview Process

Your active pursuit of relevant leads has paid off and you have been invited for an interview. To prepare, it will be helpful to know a bit about the structure of the interview process. The following sections provide information about some types of interviews that you might encounter; it's not unusual that the hiring process will involve more than one interview, so you may experience several different interview styles while pursuing the same job lead. It's also important to recognize the distinct stages in the hiring process; later in this section, you'll find tips on how to create a great impression before the interview begins, during the interview, and after it ends.

Types of Interviews

Interview styles and formats vary greatly depending on the purpose, stage of the interview process, sector or industry, and each interviewer's skills and preferences. There are many good books and websites to help with interview preparation. This section will be limited to a brief overview of the most common types of interviews: screening and assessment, panel, telephone or video, situational or targeted behavioral, and group.

Knowing the type of interview to expect and, ideally, a bit about the interviewers will help you prepare for your interview and showcase your relevant talents. Take time to research this crucial background information by connecting with others who have recently been hired or interviewed by the organizations you have been invited to interview with. If you don't have relevant contacts, take a few minutes to gather relevant details from the individual who scheduled your interview. Ask whether you will be interviewed individually or with a group, by a panel or a single interviewer. Clarify the interview process: Is this a screening interview? Will there be any assessments? If successful in this interview, what are the next steps? If there will be a series of interviews, how many interviews are typical? Who is involved in the interview process: coworkers? The hiring manager? A recruiter? A member of the HR team? Don't be afraid to ask questions; there is such variance in interview formats that you can't possibly know what to expect without asking someone.

Your first interview with an employer is likely to be for screening and assessment purposes to confirm that the claims on your resume are accurate. You may not even realize that you are being interviewed; screening may happen right at the booth at a career fair in what seems to be a completely casual and unfocused conversation with the recruiter. Similarly, later in the process, you may be invited to lunch or a social event; although such meetings may not seem like a real interview, it's important to recognize that all interactions with potential job candidates influence the decision-making process.

Expect a screening interview to include questions about your resume, past experience, and education. There may be questions to assess your knowledge or skills (i.e., an informal or semi-structured assessment process). There may also be formal or standardized assessments to complete; these could be to assess job-specific skills such as word-processing speed and accuracy and business math; soft skills such as critical thinking, honesty, and time orientation; or personal style preferences to assess fit for a specific role or team. Some interview assessments involve work simulations; for example, an "in-basket" exercise is quite typical for assessing how managers juggle priorities. Other assessments are administered by external organizations; for example, a specific driver's license or safety certificate might be required before applicants will be "promoted" to the next interview stage.

In a global economy supported by technology, and especially in the physical distancing phase of the global pandemic, it is increasingly likely that one or more steps in the interview process will be conducted by e-mail, telephone, or online. You may be asked to complete some online assessments prior to an interview, or you may need to dial in to a teleconference or web-based meeting room (e.g., GoToMeeting) or log on to a "voice-over-Internet provider (VOIP)" (e.g., Skype or Zoom). Just as you would be sure to allow extra time to get to an in-person interview, allow time to test out the technology and ensure it is working smoothly for you. If you are having any challenges, do not hesitate to ask for help. The person who set up the interview is likely quite comfortable guiding applicants through the process.

Of course, it is almost certain that you will also be interviewed in person, either by an individual or a panel of interviewers. There are significant differences between these two types of interviews. In an individual interview, you need to develop rapport with, and ultimately impress and persuade, one person. In a panel, on the other hand, rapport building and making a positive impression is more challenging; it's quite possible that the interviewers come from diverse professional backgrounds, have very different personal styles, and may even have conflicting ideas about the personal characteristics of an ideal candidate. In either case, it's important that your responses are customized to the interviewer(s)' knowledge of the sector and your occupation in particular. Recruiters and human resource professionals may be highly skilled in interviewing for interpersonal and transferable skills but may not have in-depth industry or job-specific knowledge. The hiring manager or a potential coworker, on the other hand, may have very specific questions about your technical expertise and ability to fit in with the established team.

Cultural differences can also impact your interview success. In each interview, be aware of differing culture-based expectations about level of formality (e.g., use of first or last names, professional titles), deference to age, eye contact, personal space, small talk, and the importance of group versus individual accomplishments. If you know in advance the cultural affiliations of your interviewers, cultural informants (i.e., people in your net-work who are from, or have significant experience with, different cultural backgrounds) may be helpful in alerting you to potential considerations. However, more likely, you'll have to make adjustments as you become aware of the interviewer's cultural expectations such as shaking hands when a hand is extended, standing until you are asked to sit down, or responding to small talk initiated by others.

Some interviews will require you to respond to hypothetical situations (e.g., "What would you do if ... ?"). More commonly, interviewers will be inter-ested in what you actually did under similar circumstances (e.g., "Think about a time that _____ happened. What did you do when ... ?"). These are known as "targeted-behavioral" interviews, and they are based on an underlying belief that the best predictor of future behavior is past behavior. Although it's generally much easier to engage in hypothetical discussions about ideal situations, these tend to provide "book answers" and may not represent your real-world attitudes and behaviors. Targeted-behavioral interviews, on the other hand, provide opportunities for you to share real examples of how you handled a challenge, crisis, conflict, or even an every-day workplace occurrence.

To prepare for targeted-behavioral questions, review your work, school, and general life experiences and identify two or three great "stories" that you want to incorporate into your interview. You may find it helpful to write highlights of each story using the STAR (situation, task, action, result) model. Although you likely won't refer to your written story during the interview, the act of writing it out will help refresh your memory with the details and make the example easier to recall during the interview. As the point of a STAR story is to provide evidence of how you work, ensure that the majority of the time spent telling your story is on your action (the A in STAR). Briefly describe the situation (allocate less than 10% of the story time); similarly, minimize your description of the task. However, spend about 75% of your time describing your role in the scenario, including how you made the decision about what to do and why. Finally, briefly summarize your story with a memorable ending, highlighting the result and how it was directly linked to your actions. Some stories don't have perfect endings; in those cases, wrap up the story with what you learned from the experience and how it has impacted your approach to work since.

ACTIVITY 14.2 *STAR Stories Revisited*

As you prepare for your job interview, use the space provided to anchor two or three STAR stories. For example, Steve chose to share a story about an innovative solution he developed that helped to cut pollution emissions. He chose this story strategically as it demonstrated a clear link between his extensive experience as a boilermaker and his goal to reposition his career in the green economy. In telling his story, he described how he researched the possibilities by reading some technical articles and consulting with three people from different companies. He used his network of coworkers, previous instructors from his boilermaker training, and a past supervisor who had moved on to a new company to identify his consultants, created a good rapport with each of them, and then compared and contrasted their insights with the technical research he'd done and developed a plan (action/attitude). He designed and built an adaptation to their existing equipment that effectively cut 25% of pollution emissions (result).

ELEMENT/ INTERVIEW TIME	STAR STORY #1	STAR STORY #2
Situation 10%		
Task 10%		

ELEMENT/ INTERVIEW TIME	STAR STORY #1	STAR STORY #2
Action/attitude 75%		
Result 5%		

Many organizations use a series of interviews to inform their employee selection process. Perhaps beginning with a screening interview, then an assessment interview, followed by a panel interview, this process allows potential employers to see job applicants under diverse circumstances, often on several different days. Generally, each stage in the process further shortlists the candidate pool; it is usually the interviews near the end of the series that involve more senior members of the organization.

One increasingly popular type of interview involves bringing a group of candidates in at the same time. This can be disconcerting if you're not expecting it. However, it generally serves one of two purposes: (a) an efficient way to provide much of the standard interview information typically covered in the first interview or (b) an opportunity to see how you interact with a group of peers. If the purpose is efficiency, there is little you need to do except show up on time and look appropriate for the job. In this type of interview, the group format is simply to save interviewers' time so they are not repeating the same 10 minutes of information about the organization or the hiring process with each new candidate. However, if you realize the purpose is to facilitate interaction—for example, after you arrive at the interview you are divided into groups and given a task to work on together—the best approach is to pretend you are already working for the organization and this is your project team. It is important to showcase your skills and knowledge, but not by discrediting or shaming another member of the team. Work cooperatively, share creative ideas, and take on the leadership role as appropriate.

Stages in the Interview Process

When most people hear the word *interview* they think of the specific time they will be meeting directly with the interviewers. However, the interview process actually extends over a much longer period than that. This section provides tips and strategies for preparing for the interview (the pre-interview stage), managing successfully during the interview itself, and effectively using time after the interview for reflection and follow-up.

The pre-interview stage begins even before you apply for a job. Your networking, research, and job search activities generated a lead that seemed worth pursuing. The hiring manager or selection committee agreed; you seem like a good potential fit and you have been invited for an interview. This is important to keep in mind; any time you have been called for an interview, someone has already determined that you are suitable for the position (i.e., they already like you!).

As mentioned earlier, documenting some of your initial research can save you considerable time as you prepare for an interview. Keep good job search files; bookmark the websites of the organizations you have applied to, and keep track of your contacts (Who do you know who knows something about this organization?). Before your interview, revisit the website and review your notes about the organization and the specific opening. Connect with your contacts; let them know you have been called for an interview, ask them questions you have about the organization or interview process, and request permission to use their names as references.

Using the STAR story framework, identify three or four relevant stories you'd like to introduce during the interview. Reflect on questions that have been prob-

> **Tip** Sometimes you will be given a choice of interview times; if possible, ask for the last one.

lematic for you in the past or questions you simply hope they don't ask in the interview. Although there are countless lists of "problem questions" in books and on the Internet, the only real problem questions will be those that you don't have an acceptable answer for. The question itself isn't the problem; the problem is that your answer may reveal something you would rather the interviewers did not know.

Statistically, those interviewed last get the job far more often than others; of course, this number is skewed as, in many cases, the interview process ends once a suitable candidate has been found. Those interviewed first also have a better-than-average chance of getting the job. Interviews on Mondays and Fridays tend to result in less success; mornings are usually better than afternoons. However, if you are invited to attend an interview at a scheduled time, try to accommodate; far more important than the time or day of the week is how well you prepare for and perform during the interview. If you do have a legitimate reason why you can't attend during a requested time, be honest and express your sincere interest in being interviewed—and request an alternate appointment.

What happens as you arrive for your interview is also part of the interview process; the first impression you create is significant. There are things in your control to ensure that you make a positive first impression. Are you on time? Unflustered? Suitably dressed? Well rested? Calm and cheerful? Enthusiastic? Optimistic? Be aware that your first impression may begin long before you enter the interview room. Consider the quality of your resume and cover letter; the telephone call when you were invited to the interview; the individuals you encountered in the parking lot, elevator, or coffee shop in the lobby; and your introduction of yourself to the receptionist. All of these provide opportunities for your professionalism and personal style to shine through; they may significantly impact your interview success.

During the interview, there are several distinct phases: the opening, the body of the interview, and the closing. Understanding the expectations for each of these phases can impact your interview success.

In most cases, a warm smile and a firm handshake will get you off to a good start. Eye contact (with each interviewer if there is more than one) and a simple question about how the day has been going so far may help to establish rapport. Finding common ground will put you all at ease; consider introducing a piece of relevant information that you got from your research; for example, "I notice that you had a team in the run on Sunday; I was there with a group from our school."

Most interviews begin with "small talk," which is intended to make you, the candidate, feel comfortable. However, it can sometimes feel like the most awkward part of an interview, especially if the interviewers are not good at small talk or the candidates are not prepared for it and are looking for a hidden agenda in every question asked. Practice making small talk with friends and family members until it is comfortable and natural to keep a conversation going; avoid controversial topics such as politics or religion and specialized topics that not everyone may be able to speak comfortably about (e.g., sports, emerging technology). Keep in mind that interviewers know you may be nervous; what may surprise you is that they are likely nervous too. Making a hiring decision is a big responsibility!

If you are well prepared, the body of the interview will likely flow smoothly. Generally, the interview will focus on your knowledge, skills, and attitudes (KSAs) as they relate to the position. Consider bringing some tangible evidence of your accomplishments; if you have assembled a career portfolio, it may contain a relevant sample of your work, feedback from a client, or an article that showcases your contributions to a project. Although most employers won't be interested in reviewing your whole portfolio, bringing a few relevant components to use as examples can make your responses more memorable for interviewers.

It is important to understand that some interviews will be very structured so that scores can be compared across interview candidates, interviewers, and even remote locations. This may make the flow of the interview a bit awkward; an interviewer may ask a question that it seems like you already answered. Similar to an exam in school where you may have covered material in Question 1 that would also be useful for Question 3, it's important that you answer each question thoroughly to get full points. It is fine to address this, to make the redundancy more comfortable (e.g., "As I mentioned a few minutes ago, my experience in ..."); however, be careful not to sound frustrated at having to repeat yourself. Rather, be sure your response adds value to the overall interview and use the opportunity to share another example or to showcase a different skill.

Although there are many questions that interviewers are not legally allowed to ask in an interview—relating to age, marital status, family plans, first language, ethnic background, nationality, and so on—some interviewers haven't been trained in interview protocol, and others may ask something they are curious about without even realizing the question is illegal. It is important, from your perspective, to know that it is *not* illegal to answer an illegal question. So, if you are comfortable answering the question, the best approach may be to simply answer it graciously rather than embarrass the interviewer about his or her interviewing skills. However, if you are uncomfortable answering the question or feel that it may be used to unjustly discriminate against you, consider answering the underlying question. For example, if asking about family status or plans, the interviewer is likely concerned about your availability. Consider responding with, "I realize that with a young team, daycare issues can result in time off work. However, I am from a large, supportive family—back-up daycare has never been an issue for any of my siblings, and, I know if I ever needed it, supports would be in place for me."

There will be many nonverbal clues in your interview that indicate whether your responses are on track; use them to guide subsequent answers. For example, interviewers may be looking for key words; in a panel interview, you may notice all the panelists taking notes at the same moment. This likely indicates that your answer contained what they hoped for. On the other hand, you may notice your interviewer looking puzzled, frustrated, or disengaged. Rather than assuming you have no chance of getting the job, use such cues to get back on track. Explore the concern with a statement such as, "It seems like my last answer may have been unclear. Can you tell me a bit about that so that I can help to clarify what I meant?"

Especially in panel interviews, be careful not to ignore an individual or subgroup. Although this is likely to be unintentional, review of thousands of mock interview tapes revealed that women as interviewers were acknowledged far less frequently than men. While interviewees typically responded graciously when the female interviewers asked specific questions, the women were almost completely ignored the rest of the time—something to watch for.

The end of the interview is one of the most important parts because final impressions are long lasting. Generally, an interview concludes with the interviewer asking, "Do you have any questions?" At this point, control of the interview has been handed to you, so make wise use of the opportunity. If some of the questions you prepared before the interview haven't been answered, ask them now; your questions might relate to the future direction of the organization or specific department (e.g., What changes are expected in the department over the next year?) or something that's particularly important to you (e.g., What kinds of professional development opportunities does the organization offer?). However, if all your questions have already been answered, use this time to introduce relevant information that wasn't covered during the interview and to reconfirm your interest in the job. Leave an articulate and enthusiastic final impression.

Although the actual interview has ended, the interview process will continue until a final decision has been made and an offer has been extended to (and accepted by) the successful candidate. Be sure to follow up the interview with a thank-you note or e-mail; it's not uncommon that the person who follows up is the one who gets offered the job. Sometimes you will reflect on a better answer to one of the interview questions; you could expand on that response in a follow-up note. You may also have referred to an article or website during the interview; your follow-up could include a copy of the article or a web link. If significant time goes by between an interview and a decision, you might also follow up with relevant updates such as certificates or courses now complete, changes in availability, or new contact information. Following up in a way that is meaningful (and not simply pestering the potential employer) helps to keep your name and application at the top of the list.

However, do not stop your job search just because you have had a good interview; actively continuing your search may generate even better opportunities. Having several offers to choose from can make you a more attractive candidate to a potential employer and may tip the scales in terms of prompting an offer or negotiating a good compensation package. It is not necessary to accept a job offer the moment it is made; ask when the employer needs your decision and use that time to consult with family and mentors, compare the position to your self-assessment results, and reconnect with other potential employers to see if they are close to making a decision.

Optimism has been linked to both career success and job satisfaction (Neault, 2002). However, when it comes to generating leads and reflecting on job interviews, it's important to temper optimism with pragmatism. Although it may be tempting to hold out for the perfect job, sometimes accepting a less-than-perfect opportunity positions you well for next steps. With additional experience and an expanded network, you might be considered for internal openings or may be successful the next time you apply for a job that is just slightly out of reach right now.

With interview success comes a career transition, sometimes within an organization and sometimes to a new organization and perhaps a new region. The next section will help you navigate career transitions as you encounter them.

Supporting Transitions to Next Career Stages

There are many transitional periods in life where career planning takes on increased importance; some of these include school-to-work transitions, life role transitions, health challenges that necessitate a change in work responsibilities, and relocation. Although some transitions such as graduation are long anticipated, others, such as a layoff, are unexpected and involuntary. Some economic shifts such as those brought about by the global COVID-19 pandemic have unprecedented, widespread consequences. All transitions, however, can be challenging, exhilarating, unsettling, or refreshing; they can positively or negatively impact the sense of hope that is at the center of the hope-action approach. Several career management specialists have developed models to help put career transitions in perspective. Two of those models are presented here.

Bridges Transition Model

William Bridges (2004) described change as an external *event* and transition as an internal *process*. His transition model identifies three distinct stages—the ending, a neutral zone, and the new beginning—but he also addresses the pretransition stage as it can be an important time of anticipation and preparation.

Bridges suggested that tasks must be completed in each of the stages before the overall transition process can be successfully concluded. Tasks in the ending stage relate primarily to closure, for example, studying for and writing final exams, submitting term papers, applying for graduation, and giving notice to a landlord that you will be moving out. In the neutral zone, there may be a frenzy of chaotic activity as you explore possibilities and make new plans. However, there may also be quiet times of reflection, self-assessment, recovery, and waiting. The neutral zone has been described as a bit like walking on quicksand: not very stable or secure. The new beginning is marked by feeling settled, regaining a sense of confidence and competence as you reestablish your life and career.

ACTIVITY 14.3 *Transitioning Through the Three Zones*

Use the table to list tasks, anticipated challenges, and potential supports for each of the stages in the Bridges transition model: ending, neutral zone, and new beginning. For example, in the ending stage, Steve will need to adjust to being home full time and take time to grieve the loss of a job and a lifestyle that he'd really enjoyed. Steve will transition to the neutral zone once he finds options for alternate childcare arrangements and learns more about work that he could potentially do within the green economy; his challenge will be making new contacts, especially while physical distancing is a requirement due to the pandemic. However, he is active on social media and has some good contacts to start with. His experience with the air pollution abatement system gives him a good starting place for finding common ground in discussions with people interested in the green economy. Steve's new beginning will involve identifying a new employer and possibly some additional training or certifications. It's possible that they'll need to relocate as a family. He anticipates some tensions as the family adjusts to a change in employment and potentially relocating, but they are excited that he will be moving toward work that will have more regular hours and not involve flying in to remote camps for days at a time.

STAGE	SPECIFIC TASKS	ANTICIPATED CHALLENGES	POTENTIAL SUPPORTS
Ending			

Neutral			
Beginning			

Roller Coaster Model

Borgen and Amundson (1987) used a roller coaster metaphor to highlight the emotional reactions associated with job loss and unemployment; these reactions are quite similar to stages of grief or mourning, such as one experiences with other kinds of loss (e.g., loss of a loved one or loss of one's health). In the case example, Steve's story exemplifies this roller coaster as he reports feeling both excited about moving into a new sector but sad about leaving work and a lifestyle that he'd enjoyed. Searching for work can be a bit like paddling in whitewater, with emotions rapidly shifting from exhilaration (being selected for an interview) to despair (not being short-listed for a second one) to optimism (as a new opportunity surfaces that seems just right).

Both of these transition models acknowledge that transition is a process. A wide range of concerns and emotional reactions is normal during transitions. Being prepared for them by strengthening your supports and coping resources will help you successfully position yourself for the next stage in your career. Generating specific work opportunities will take time and emotional investment; starting as early as possible will facilitate an effective transition.

Summary

Actively engaging in job search can take considerable time; typically, it also signals the beginning of a transition. Be sure not to leave this important stage to the last minute. Effective career management is ongoing, so it is always a good idea to be nurturing your network and generating potential leads.

Steve, introduced at the beginning of this chapter, will have a particularly challenging time generating leads as he has been laid off during a global pandemic that has impacted work across sectors and left many skilled people unemployed at the same time. Also, within their family, it is convenient for him to be home and helping with childcare at this specific time—resulting in less time for making new career plans and for job searching. Making the basic decisions about the type of work he'd like to do and when he'd prefer to start needs to be his first step; just as it's impossible to navigate efficiently without a destination in mind, it is essential to know where your career is headed before actively beginning the work search and interview process.

This chapter has provided strategies for generating concrete work opportunities, tips for how to network effectively, information about types of interviews and stages of the interview process, and an overview of the transition process. Use the questions provided to reflect on your learning from this chapter and take it to a deeper level through discussion.

Questions for Reflection and Discussion

1. Steve is in the midst of multiple transitions: unexpected job loss, more time at home, temporarily taking on childcare responsibilities, and reflecting on how he'd prefer to reposition his career. Which of the transition models might be most helpful for Steve? What transitions are you going through? Which model or models are most helpful for you?

2. Generating specific job leads is likely to be challenging for Steve as he is interested in leaving the oil and gas sector and joining the green economy. What recommendations would you give him for next steps in generating leads? How is Steve's situation similar to or different from yours? What can you do right now to generate specific job leads?

3. Everyone has some questions that they hope won't be asked in a job interview. What do you suppose Steve is dreading being asked? How might you help him prepare for those questions? What questions are you dreading and why? Brainstorm ways to effectively answer your problem questions.

References

Borgen, W. A., & Amundson, N. E. (1987). The dynamics of unemployment. *Journal for Counseling & Development, 66*, 180–184. https://doi.org/10.1002/j.1556-6676.1987.tb00841.x

Bridges, W. (2004). *Transitions: Making sense of life's changes* (2nd ed.). Cambridge, MA: Da Capo Press.

Krumboltz, J. D. (2011). Capitalizing on happenstance. *Journal of Employment Counseling, 48*(4). 156–158. https://doi.org/10.1002/j.2161-1920.2011.tb01101.x

Neault, R. A. (2002). Thriving in the new millennium: Career management in the changing world of work. *Canadian Journal of Career Development, 1*(1), 11–21.

Additional Resources

Bahler, K. (2018). 5 questions you'll hear at your next job interview—and exactly how to answer them. *Money, 47*(8), 23–25

> Describes common questions and strategies for answering them effectively without sounding over rehearsed.

LiveCareer Staff Writer. (n.d.). *The 150 typical job interview questions*. LiveCareer. https://www.livecareer.com/interview/questions/interview-questions

> A comprehensive database of traditional and behavioral interview questions to spur your thinking about what you might encounter during an interview.

Pankratz, R. (2016). Mobile technology: Evolutions and trends for career resources, searches, and networking. *Career Planning & Adult Development Journal, 32*(3), 58–61.

> Provides insights into how mobile technology is being used by organizations and job seekers as well as how professionals are utilizing technology to network.

Schawbel, D. (2011, May 23). *Social networking for career success*. Forbes. https://www.forbes.com/sites/danschawbel/2011/05/23/social-networking-for-career-success/

> A thoughtful interview with Miriam Salpeter, co-editor of Personal Branding Magazine and owner of Keppie Careers, a coaching and consulting firm. Salpeter speaks to the role of social media and shares career tips for Twitter.

Tan, J. K., Teoh, M. L., & Tan S. K. (2016). Beyond "greeting" and "thanking": Politeness in job interviews. *3L: Southeast Asian Journal of English Language Studies, 22*(3), 171–184. https://doi.org/10.17576/3L-2016-2203-12

> Examines strategies for making a positive impression on the employers during job interviews, specifically politeness. Noticing and attending to interviewers' interests, wants, needs, or goods and raising/asserting common grounds to establish solidarity were identified as positive politeness strategies. Requesting for clarification or repetition was identified as a negative politeness strategy.

15 ADAPTING AT PRESENT AND FUTURE MOMENTS

OBJECTIVES

This chapter focuses on the need to adapt when changes emerge through work or life events. After reading and completing activities in this chapter, you will be able to do the following:

- Increase your awareness of some of the social and economic trends that might impact your career decision making

- Understand how to apply a "creating" stance to problems that you are facing

CASE EXAMPLE

Edward is finishing his degree in psychology, graduating early (end of year) because he completed some summer classes. During his school years he had a part-time job in a youth program run by correctional services. When he thinks about his career planning, he knows that he prefers working in a hectic environment. He enjoys the challenge of multitasking and likes to be doing work that is making a difference. At the end of his program he talks to his manager about future career options. There is every likelihood of a full-time job coming up in the new fiscal year (starting in April), and he is obviously in a great position to qualify for this opportunity. It is suggested that he work part time during the summer and then when the job comes up he can apply for it. He also has an opportunity to take a 3-year contract position working for an employment counseling agency. This position would start right away.

In assessing the situation Edward decides that he really would like to wait for the correctional service position. During the break he might be able to take that Australian trip that he has been dreaming about. The only problem is lack of finances, but he can get a short-term loan and pay the money back when he starts working in April. Edward manages to get the funds for his trip and heads off on a 3-month trip. Unfortunately, toward the end of his trip, while in Perth he receives an e-mail message from his former manager advising him that because of the pandemic there have been cutbacks and the position that he had counted on is no longer a possibility. This is obviously shocking news, but there is little he can do about it. He decides to come home and look for other work.

Social and Economic Trends

There certainly are significant social and economic realities that need to be considered during this current upheaval. It is difficult to predict how everything will change, but one can be assured that there certainly will be a new social and economic landscape. Listed below are some of the trends that we have identified:

1. Communication and information technology will continue to play an important function. This does not mean that everyone needs to be a computer programmer, but there will be the expectation that you are able to use computers, word processing, cell phones, and so on.

2. There are no "safe" jobs where you can expect to spend your entire career. The idea of staying with one firm and working your way "up the ladder" no longer applies. Your focus needs to be on learning and improving your employability skills. When you have reached the limit of what a job can offer you, it will be time to move on and look for other opportunities. Sometimes this will mean acquiring additional education to assist you in taking the next step.

3. In many situations people will need to consider options other than the traditional full-time job with security. This means being willing to explore a portfolio career with elements of part-time work, contract work, and self-employment options..

4. In positioning oneself for the challenging economic times, it is helpful to think about new social trends such as people working more

from home, a greater focus on healthy living, security issues, and environmental concerns.

5. Workers will generally need higher levels of critical thinking and skill training. This means that it is important to seek education where critical thinking and skill development are highlighted.

6. Lifelong learning needs to be incorporated into your long-term plan. There is the expectation that you will keep learning while you are working. There also may be periods of time when you need to step outside of the workforce to acquire additional training.

7. Organizations are restructuring, and as a result there are often fewer numbers of middle-management positions. Organizations also are impacted by mergers and downsizing. To stay afloat in the midst of turbulence you need to be flexible and focus on your own need to keep growing your employability skills.

8. Employment opportunities will vary widely from region to region, and to take advantage of emerging possibilities you may need to consider working online or moving to other parts of the country.

9. Despite all your best efforts you may find yourself facing periods of underemployment or even unemployment. This is just the new reality, and you need to stay hopeful and be prepared for more economic instability.

10. In such turbulence it is important to remain true to yourself and your own personal and family needs. The choices you make should be grounded in personal health and integrity (Amundson et al., 2009; Herr, 1999; Storey, 2000).

Plans Interrupted: The Nature of Life

Hopefully the list of trends has not generated any undue anxiety. It is meant to help you prepare yourself for what lies ahead. The world is complex, and there is a great deal of uncertainty. It is important to have plans but also recognize that these plans may be interrupted by life circumstances. There are many people who are still operating on "yesterday's story." It is essential to understand that you need to become more proactive in directing your own career development. Rather than just letting it happen, you need to have a vision of what you want to create for yourself and be prepared to play an active role in creating your own opportunities.

Edward, from the case example in this chapter, returned to North America and restarted his job search. His friend's father owns a landscaping business, so that is one option that emerges. He would make good money at this work, and it will help him get out of debt. There also is another temporary position that has opened with correctional services. The only problem is that this job doesn't pay as well, it is with a different population (older workers), and it also involves relocation—a small town several hours away from his current location. The job also does not have the same high energy level that was part of his previous experience. Edward decided to take the longer view and took the correctional job. He worked hard and within six months was offered a full-time position in a larger city. In this case there was a happy ending without too much hardship. In reflecting on this experience, Edward realized that he was very fortunate to have such a quick resolution to this challenge. He also realized that it was a good move to stay true to himself and take the longer view. There are many people who jump too quickly and end up doing work that pays the bills but doesn't offer much satisfaction.

A starting point in directing your own career is to understand what you really enjoy (your passions). With so much uncertainty all around you, it is essential to have some form of anchor to rely on; otherwise, you will be flip-flopping from one situation to the other without regard to your own personal needs, interests, and talents.

The Problem With Problem Solving

As you contemplate social and labor market changes and your own situation it is very easy to be filled with apprehension and anxiety. In many ways finding work has become much more challenging. So, how does one approach the situation in a way that strengthens personal power and minimizes some of the anxiety associated with uncertainty? Perhaps some of the difficulty is the way in which we frame the problem.

Let's begin with a short exercise.

ACTIVITY 15.1 *Creating Versus Problem Solving*

1. Take a moment and think about a difficult problem in your life (it may be the issue of finding work) and how you need to problem solve the solution. What are your thoughts and feelings when you focus on a problem in this way?

a. Thoughts

b. Feelings

2. Now, take a deep breath and shift to something that you'd love to create—something that you would love to make happen but haven't yet had the opportunity to realize your dream. What thoughts and feelings are associated with this scenario?

a. Thoughts

b. Feelings

Many people when they are in a problem-solving mode feel discouraged, overwhelmed, anxious, dispirited, hopeless, and so on. When they are in creative mode they feel energized, hopeful, excited about the possibilities, and ready to make it happen.

Robert Fritz (1989) in his classic book *The Path of Least Resistance* outlines the advantages of seeking a pathway with a heart. Bruce Elkin (2003) takes this further and illustrates how creativity is a more effective way of handling life challenges. He identifies the following flaws with a problem-solving approach and suggests that these flaws "prevent problem solving from consistently producing real and lasting results" (p. 62):

1. Problem solving often focuses on finding the right answer (a convergent approach). But what if the answer is more complex and does not lend itself easily to a single answer? In this scenario a more creative approach allows for divergence and the flexibility that one needs in solving problems.

2. When you are in a problem-solving mode you often start from a weaker emotional position (e.g., discouraged, anxious, and helpless). From a creative stance there is more positive energy and excitement about what might be possible.

3. Problem solving often emphasizes temporary solutions that can be unsatisfactory in the long run. With a creative perspective there is always a focus on what one ultimately wants to create, and even when there are challenges these are viewed as temporary setbacks to the ultimate result.

4. When you are problem solving you are usually generating actions and results that are either viewed as "winning" or "losing." In a more complex world it can be helpful to remove the either-or categories and view what is happening as part of a longer-term plan.

Elkin (2003) suggests that problem solving often leads to simplistic answers that don't fit well with our complex society. He also indicates that being creative is a more powerful motivating force than problem solving.

ACTIVITY 15.2 *Applying a Creating Approach*

When it comes to viewing your own situation, take a moment to see if you can apply a more creative stance to the future that you would like to create for yourself. Rather than being bombarded by negativity, start from a position of hope, strength, creativity. Answer the following questions:

What matters to you and what type of life would you like to create for yourself?

What needs to be done in order to get there, to make this a reality?

What is the first step that you need to take?

Tip When you are facing a difficult situation, make a conscious effort to focus on your strengths. Think about a range of possibilities and try to be creative in developing strategies for success.

Summary

These are uncertain times. There will be unexpected challenges and problems to be faced. In facing these problems it is helpful to adopt a "creating" stance. With this approach there is the possibility of attaining greater energy and enthusiasm for the task at hand and also learning to think broadly about possible solutions.

In preparing for a more turbulent social and economic situation there are challenges such as unemployment, underemployment, mergers and downsizing, and personal life issues that might need to be faced. While these challenges present some real-life/career barriers, they are not insurmountable.

Questions for Reflection and Discussion

1. What are your thoughts about how Edward handled his situation? In responding to this question think about some of the social and economic trends.

2. Can you apply some of these trends to your situation?

3. How would adopting a "creating" approach to career search change the way you think and feel about the process?

References

Amundson, N. E., Harris-Bowlsbey, J., & Niles, S. G. (2009). *Essential elements of career counseling: Processes and techniques* (2nd ed.). Pearson.

Elkin, B. (2003). *Simplicity and success.* Trafford Press.

Fritz R. (1989). *The path of least resistance.* Columbine.

Herr, E. L. (1999). *Counseling in a dynamic society: Contexts and practices for the 21st century.* American Counseling Association.

Storey, J. (2000). "Fracture lines" in the career environment. In A. Collins & R. Young (Eds.), *The future of career* (pp. 21–36). Cambridge University Press.

We are excited about the work you have done! The time and energy you have devoted to using Hope-Action Theory will be rewarded many times over. Keep developing the awareness and skill sets we have shared with you. Your main job in life is to be the best you that you can be. The approach we teach in this book will help lead you to your best, true, and most authentic self. We encourage you to return time and again to Hope-Action Theory. As you learn more about yourself and the world, as well as your place in it, the theory will continue to be an important reference for you. We cannot wait to learn more about how you have used this book to create careers full of hope, satisfaction, and enjoyment.

INDEX

Printed in the USA
CPSIA information can be obtained
at www.ICGtesting.com
LVHW070303191023
761494LV00021B/136